THREE-DIMENSIONAL DISCIPLESHIP

*The Height, Breadth & Depth of the
Life God Created You to Live*

R. SCOTT RODIN
WITH MELINDA DELAHOYDE,
WILLIAM HIGH & PAT MCCOWN

KINGDOM LIFE PUBLISHING

PRAISE FOR
THREE-DIMENSIONAL DISCIPLESHIP

"*Three-Dimensional Discipleship* is a refreshing book focused on moving us beyond simply producing fruit for Christ—to living extraordinary, radically altered lives—life in the zone. The subject is timely. The substance is transforming."

DAN BUSBY, President, Evangelical Council for Financial Accounatbility

"This is a great book that connects with and challenges Christ-followers at all stages of maturity. Its foundation of inarguable Biblical truth and the depth and authenticity of the testimonies makes for an impactful, refreshing, convicting, and compelling read that properly honors the Architect and Source of our sanctification and the fruit we might increasingly bear along the way. The call to greater intimacy with Christ as the source to "bearing" fruit (versus "producing" in our own strength) is spot-on for those desiring to be Christ's stewards and servant leaders in their work, families, and communities. This compact but deeply beneficial book reflects the truth that—no matter our position or standing among men—our life is but a vapor in eternal terms, and that apart from Christ we can do nothing that truly matters for eternity. I look forward to sharing it with many others in the months ahead!"

DON BAREFOOT, AFC, President & CEO, C12 Group

"Imagine hearing the words, "Well done good and faithful servant." This book will surprise you as it describes the kind of person who will hear those words. I will refer to this book often as I examine my own life and coach leaders around the world."

KURT DILLINGER, President, Life International

"This is a thought-provoking look at the answers to two important questions; 'what is driving you?' and 'are you a steward or an owner?' Then, it reveals how your answer to these questions will impact how you love your neighbor. I can assure you that you will look at life and others differently after you read this book."

DAVID WILLS, President, National Christian Foundation

"This message is desperately needed—especially for those of us who want to be found faithful to our callings. These "mentors in stewardship" are faithful guides. I found my soul singing with the authors as they unpacked what "abiding in Christ" looks like in their lives and ministries. These pages shine with the insight that comes from intimacy with Christ that overflows with lasting personal impact for our own walk, and the magnetizing of others' to follow Christ. I encourage you to accept their invitation to "Come, and abide in Christ and watch His fruit multiply in and through your life."

LARRY GADBAUGH, CEO, Pregnancy Resource Centers of Greater Portland

"What does DEEP discipleship look like? This book provides a multi-dimensional structure to plumb the depths of discipleship. Accessible yet challenging.....read it and grow!"

PATRICK JOHNSON, Chief Architect, Generous Church

Kingdom Life Publishing
P.O. Box 389
Colbert, WA 99005

All Scripture quotations, unless otherwise indicated, are taken from the Holy Bible, New International Version, NIV. Copyright © 1973, 1978, 1984 by International Bible Society. All rights reserved.

ISBN 978-0-9834727-5-9

Printed in the United States of America

Contents

INTRODUCTION:

The Discipleship Zone

Some people call it being in "the flow," "the groove," or "the game." The most common term for this phenomenon is being in "the zone."

Theories and applications of being in the zone and its relationship with athletic competitive advantage are studied in the field of sport psychology. According to psychologist Mihaly Csíkszentmihályi, "*flow* is the mental state of operation in which a person in an activity is fully immersed in a feeling of energized focus, full involvement, and success in the process of the activity."[1] For some of us, this may be such a rare occurrence that we can hardly relate to it. However, for athletes and performers this term defines a place where performance, and the pure joy derived from it, are unequaled. It is, as Daniel Goleman states in his book *Emotional Intelligence: Why It Can Matter More Than IQ*, "a single-minded immersion and represents perhaps the ultimate in harnessing the emotions in

1. Csikszentmihalyi, Mihaly. *Flow: The Psychology of Optimal Experience.* New York: Harper and Row, 1990.

the service of performing and learning. In flow the emotions are not just contained and channeled, but positive, energized, and aligned with the task at hand."[2]

Baseball players in this state will comment that the baseball looks like a cantaloupe when they are up to bat. They see the ball better than they have ever seen it before, and hitting it becomes automatic, and pure joy. Golfers refer to it as being in "the slot," every swing finding that perfect arc, and hands and wrists and eyes all connecting in one effortless motion. Basketball players know they have made the shot before it leaves their hands. Tennis players have mentally returned a serve before their opponent has tossed the ball in the air. For other performers, the experience is the same. Pianists witness to an almost out of body experience as they watch their hands float across the keys in a semi-detached state of euphoria. Actors lose themselves in their character to such an extent that they momentarily forget who they are. Even writers can become so singularly focused on their work that they cannot type fast enough to capture their thoughts, and hours fly by like seconds. In every sport or artistic endeavor, there is a "sweet spot" that is coveted.

We know when we are in it, and we know when we are not. Getting in it requires focus and concentration combined with a willingness to let go of mechanics and

2. Goleman, Daniel. *Emotional Intelligence: Why It Can Matter More Than IQ*. Bantam Books, 1996, p. 91.

techniques and allow natural abilities and pure energy to take over. Getting out of it usually involves distraction, loss of concentration, and the shifting of our focus from the natural to the mechanical.

Life outside the zone is hard. Baseballs look like golf balls, and golf balls look like marbles. Our swings become stiff and mechanical as we focus on every small movement and try to correct every slight error. We become a bundle of nerves and seem constantly distracted by everything except that which we are trying to accomplish. The result is not only poor performance but also anxiety, stress, frustration, and despair. Ask a baseball player who is hitting below .200, a golfer with the shanks, or an author with writer's block.

It seems that from a physiological and psychological standpoint we were created to operate in the zone. If the ultimate human experience includes peak performance and deep joy, then we were meant to spend the majority of our lives in the zone. Our thesis in this little book is that the same is true for our walk with Jesus Christ.

Defining The Zone In Discipleship Terms

We believe that there is a zone for Christians. It is a place where we live more fully for Jesus Christ than anywhere else and experience the greatest joy as a result. Most of the saints knew it. If you read the biographies and writings of the great sages of the Christian church, you'll find in them a consistent testimony to their way of life that seemed to defy their own personal circumstances and the condition of the world around them. It was as if so many of the saints lived in a slightly altered state of reality that allowed them to exhibit Christlike qualities in every situation in life.

We see the same sense of alternative reality in the lives of so many of the biblical heroes and heroines. Alongside their deeply flawed character and sinful nature, we see their faith carry them into a state where nothing outside of them seemed to have any impact on their sense of purpose and inner peace. Daniel spent a peaceful night with ravenous lions. Paul sang praises to God from the depths of a dark prison on the night before he was to be executed. Shadrach, Meshach, and Abednego went willingly into the fiery furnace. Stephen looked to the heavens in rapture as stones were beating his body to death.

How do we understand such detached responses to such jarringly real experiences? From where does the strength and perspective come to walk through life in a state of peace and contentment amid a world of sharp, jagged edges and naked wires?

We believe the answer is woven through scripture, bearing witness to the life Christ came to inaugurate for all of us as children of the triune God of grace. It starts with the person of Jesus Christ. There is a quasi-mysterious nature to the life Christ lived. It is as if he were tuned into a different mental frequency than the people around him. He asked different questions, relied on a different source of strength and power, and moved in an alternate state of wellbeing and grace. He lived this way while being fully human. He was one of many itinerant rabbis of his day, just a Jewish boy with little training from a low-class family in a local town. But his presence drew people to him because he carried an aura about him that bore witness to a connection with God that no one else seemed to have—not the Pharisees, not the priests, not the Romans, nor the Sanhedrin. Jesus was a man who lived in a zone of power and grace. He could tap an unknown well of love and forgiveness that shocked and offended some and set many others free. And those near him sensed a power that, while almost always restrained, was somehow connected to the armies of heaven itself.

> There is a quasi-mysterious nature to the life Christ lived. It is as if he were tuned into a different mental frequency than the people around him. He asked different questions, relied on a different source of strength and power, and moved in an alternate state of wellbeing and grace. He lived this way while being fully human.

As followers of Christ, we are called to a life of participation in the perfect life that was lived already for us. We have the honor and the obligation to embrace this life as Christ did.

We have been promised the mind of Christ (1 Corinthians 2:16). We are the body of Christ (1 Corinthians 12:27). It is Christ who lives in us (Romans 8:11), Christ who is making his appeal through us (2 Corinthians 5:20), and Christ who all others should see in us (John 17:20–26). As disciples of Jesus Christ, we are to live as he lived, and that means being disciples who experience life in the zone.

> The zone is exactly where Christ wants us to be. It is the intersection of three dimensions of the Christian worldview that free us, empower us, and enable us to live for Christ like never before.

What Jesus promises to those of us who follow him is an extraordinary, radically altered way of living. It includes peace, not as the world gives (John 14:27), abundant life that the thief cannot steal or destroy (John 10:10), life that is truly life (1 Timothy 6:19), peace that passes all understanding (Philippians 4:7), and truth that sets us free (John 8:32). This is the most uncommon life we can possibly imagine. It is a revolutionary departure from the ordinary, the routine, the mundane. It has a richness that few of us know but to whom each of us is called. It is life lived fully for him, life as we were created to live it, *life in the zone.*

There are three dimensions to what we are calling "the discipleship zone." Each of these has value on their own, yet when a person is able to yield themselves to all three, the combination provides for the Christian a spiritual experience like none other. The zone is exactly where Christ wants us to be. It is the intersection of three dimensions of the Christian worldview that free us, empower us, and enable us to live for Christ like never before. Our goal in this book is to describe these three dimensions and lead you through a process of disciplines that can help you experience for yourself the profound joy of living as a Christian in the zone.

The Three Dimensions:
Height, Breadth, and Depth

First, the discipleship zone has height. It is known by its ability to connect to the heavens through a humble and abiding relationship to God. We were created with a capacity for a deeper level of intimacy with God than we have ever experienced. It is there waiting for us. We were created for this, and we are called and equipped to embrace it as our own. We will develop this first dimension through a rediscovery of what it means to abide in Christ. This intimacy with God yields for us the life of height of a disciple of Jesus Christ.

Second, the discipleship zone has breadth. It is wide and all encompassing in its understanding of God's absolute ownership of everything. This simple truth has a rather staggering effect if we take it seriously. We will explore the call to move from owners to stewards in every dimension of our life, and as we do, to experience the freedom of the faithful steward. This freedom is the breadth of the disciple of Jesus Christ.

Third, the discipleship zone has depth. Following our newfound intimacy with God and our freedom as a steward of all of life, we can live with our neighbors as God intended and see them as we have never seen them before. Relationships provide the depth of our life's journey if we will see our neighbors as ends and not merely as means. We were created to bear the image of a triune God—a God who is relationship in his very nature. As we reflect that image in our relationships, we add this third, essential component to the life of a disciple of Jesus Christ.

> Living in this three-dimensional state, we experience the discipleship zone. It is a sacred place where heaven and earth seem almost to touch.

This is the three-dimensional structure of the life of a disciple who follows Jesus Christ. Living in this three-dimensional state, we experience the discipleship zone. It is a sacred place where heaven and earth seem almost to touch. It is a transcendent place where God's peace truly surpasses the situations we face on all sides. It is a solid place, a rock amid shifting sand, a sure foundation in a world of ever-crumbling moorings.

We are invited to live every moment of life in this zone. It is not meant for an occasional visit. It is not just the mountaintop euphoria or an escapist's moment of fancy. It is the absolute reality of our very existence, the DNA of a child of God in Jesus Christ.

Our prayer is that you will discover for yourself this very intimate, astonishing, and ever-present place where God and humanity dance to the sound of one heart and one spirit.

This is discipleship in three dimensions. Welcome to the zone!

HEIGHT
THE FIRST DIMENSION

Apples of Glass

R. Scott Rodin

I don't know if there's a place in your life where God has spoken to you in a powerful, life-altering way—a moment and a location where you have sensed the Spirit and the presence of God so intensely and clearly that it holds a special place in your heart. Maybe it's a mountaintop or a chapel. Maybe it's sitting by the ocean or some other wonderful, peaceful, sacred location.

I have a place in my life where, on two occasions over the past eight years, God has spoken to me in a clear, almost audible voice. It's neither a peaceful nor a memorable place. It's not scenic or serene. It is a ten-mile stretch of Interstate 90 in northern Idaho between the summit of Lookout Pass and the city of Kellogg, Idaho. I would not have expected God to speak in a "still small voice" on four lanes of asphalt. But in what is now a most sacred space, God has twice brought a word to me that has fundamentally changed my life.

The first one occurred in 2002, when I was coming down off of Lookout Pass in a twenty-four-foot moving van pulling an empty car trailer. At 75 mph (that's the speed limit, by the way), and in defiance of the safety chain, hitches, and emergency cable brake we had in place, my fifteen-hundred-pound car trailer came completely unhitched from my truck and moved over all on its own into the adjacent lane of traffic. God spoke to me that day, but that's a story for another book.

The one that I want to tell you about happened in October of 2010. Even after forty years of walking with Christ, on that October day, driving the same stretch of freeway where I lost the car trailer some eight years earlier, God spoke to me in the most powerful way that I've experienced in my entire Christian walk. What I heard and what I experienced changed my life dramatically, and it confronted me with the greatest challenge that I've faced as a Christian, and as a leader. I will be honest with you and say that I am still struggling with it today. My purpose in this chapter is to invite you into that struggle with me. In order to understand what happened at that moment on Interstate 90 somewhere in the middle of Idaho, I want to back up and tell you a little about the journey that got me there.

The Journey

I am by nature a producer. I like to get things done. I write to-do lists, strategic plans, and development plans. In my consulting role, I help not-for-profit organizations be more effective, show a better bottom line, and raise more money.

I like to write, to teach, to speak, and to do things that I know will have a tangible return. I am drawn to activities and work that allows me to point to results that affirm for me that my life is producing fruit. Most of you reading this book are probably like me, driven to produce fruit. We want to live our life so that at its end we can point to our work and say, "My life mattered. It was purposeful. I did something for the kingdom of God."

There may be many reasons for the sense of drivenness we feel, but for me it comes primarily from my reading of the parable of the talents in Matthew 25:14–30. We all know the story. A business owner prepares to go away on a business trip. He calls his three top employees in and gives them each a sum of money to invest for him while he is away. He gives the first worker five gold coins, the second two gold coins, and the third a single gold coin. He says to them each, "Take care of this while I'm gone." When he comes back from his trip, he calls them together and asks them for an accounting of what they have done with the funds he entrusted to them. The first and second employee had each invested their coins and had something to show for it, a good return that they gave over to the business owner. In response he says to them, "Well done, good and faithful servant. You've been faithful over small things, now come and enter into the joy of your master." The third worker does not fare as well. He reckoned that if he invested the money and lost it he would be in severe trouble because the business owner was a shrewd and even ruthless man, "reaping where he did not sow." So to be safe and minimize his risk, the third employee stuck the coin in a hole in the ground. When the owner returned, he was able to safely return the original coin to his boss without loss. To his likely great surprise, this was met with sharp rebuke. The risk-intolerant servant gets thrown out on his ear and loses everything.

All of my life, I have lived with the hope that I will stand before Jesus Christ on the final day and hear him say to me those precious words, "Well done, good and faithful servant. Come and share your master's happiness." Isn't that the affirmation of our entire life? If so, how do we make sure that we will hear those words and not be like the third servant who thought he had done the right things but was thrown out into darkness?

This is not about our salvation, which comes solely through grace by faith. This is about the ultimate value of our life as we seek to live it out as the obedient children of God. This is the concluding word to our entire existence, the ultimate measurement of our faithfulness in response to the perfect faithfulness of our gracious Lord and Savior. "Well done" speaks to, well, what we have *done*. Will our master be pleased with how we have invested the talents given to us in whatever form and quantity they may be? Will our life be immortalized by the eternal words of the eternal God,

"This is a life that was well-lived and pleasing to me"? That is what is at stake in this story.

I have long believed that in order to hear those words we must produce fruit and show a net gain from what we have been given. Just like the master's servants, we're called to accomplish things with what we have so that when we finally stand before God we have something to show for the talents he entrusted to us. To me that means producing fruit—lots of it!

In this fruit producer worldview, here is what that final scene of life looks like to me. I see myself standing before the Lord on the final day. He looks down and says, "Scott Rodin, what do you have to show for your life?" He is asking about how well I invested my talents for the work of the kingdom. I answer by climbing into in a semitruck, backing it up in front of Jesus (so he can see it well), and unloading crate after crate of the fruit that I have produced. As I unload each crate I say, confidently, "Jesus, I produced fruit. I produced a lot of fruit." I just keep piling it up in front of Jesus—crate after crate of stuff I have done, things I have produced, the work of my hands—so that he can see all the fruit in my life. "Look at the things that I did," I continue, "the books I wrote, the speaking and preaching I did. Look at the organizations that I led. Look at the money that we raised. Look at the strategic plans we were able to accomplish."

When all of it is finally unloaded, I see myself standing in front of the wall of creates laden with *my* fruit and saying, "Look at all the fruit I have produced, Lord. How did I do?" And then I will wait, holding my breath and praying with every ounce of energy that I will hear those glorious, affirming words in response.

I have a confession to make. I have lived my entire adult Christian life believing in my heart that when I do actually stand there and pile up all my fruit, Christ is going to look at all of it, measure it, and then turn to me with a deep sigh and say, "Well, I guess you did your best. It's probably all we could have expected." I never for a moment have had the peace in my heart that I could ever produce enough fruit.

You see, we never *can* produce enough fruit. What do you do as a fruit producer if you want to hear those words and you don't think you've produced enough fruit? You try even harder to produce more fruit! I went about looking for ways to figure out how I could produce more fruit, how I could make the grade, how I could stand in solidarity with the two faithful servants who invested the coins and had a return to show the master.

I was in this fruit-producing mindset in my devotions one summer when I came across John 15:1–17. My eyes rejoiced to read again those beautiful words:

> I am the true vine, and my Father is the gardener. He cuts off every branch in me that bears no fruit, while every branch that does bear fruit he prunes so that it will be even more fruitful. You are already clean because of the word I have spoken to you. Remain in me, as I also remain in you. No branch can bear fruit by itself; it must remain in the vine. Neither can you bear fruit unless you remain in me. I am the vine; you are the branches. If you remain in me and I in you, you will bear much fruit; apart from me you can do nothing. If you do not remain in me, you are like a branch that is thrown away and withers; such branches are picked up, thrown into the fire and burned. If you remain in me and my words remain in you, ask whatever you wish, and it will be done for you. This is to my Father's glory, that you bear much fruit, showing yourselves to be my disciples. As the Father has loved me, so I have loved you. Now remain in my love. If you keep my commands, you will remain in my love, just as I have kept my Father's commands and remain in his love. I

have told you this so that my joy may be in you and that your joy may be complete. My command is this: Love each other as I have loved you. Greater love has no one than this: to lay down one's life for one's friends. You are my friends if you do what I command. I no longer call you servants, because a servant does not know his master's business. Instead, I have called you friends, for everything that I learned from my Father I have made known to you. You did not choose me, but I chose you and appointed you so that you might go and bear fruit—fruit that will last—and so that whatever you ask in my name the Father will give you. This is my command: that you Love one another.

Coming to this text with the mindset of a fruit producer, I thought, *This might be it! This might be the secret to help me understand how I can produce enough fruit for the kingdom for my work to be acceptable in the master's sight.*

In spite of my delight at finding what seemed to be a fruit producer's dream verse, I also found that when you examine John 15 through the lens of a fruit producer, you face a couple of problems. The first one was this phrase: "apart from me you can do nothing." Frankly, I didn't buy it. I was aware that the writers of scripture sometimes use a little hyperbole to make a point. I felt this "apart from me you can do nothing" sounded like one of those things you'd expect Jesus to say, but there was probably some exaggeration at play here. To be honest with you, in my life there have been times when I have been spiritually dry, but I didn't stop going to work or doing things for the kingdom. I still produced fruit even when I felt "apart from Christ" spiritually. I could understand if he had said, "apart from me you can't do all of what you would really like to do" or "it would not be as effective." But "you can do nothing"? Without a way to reconcile the verse, I just passed that section by without too much concern.

The other problem, a much bigger problem, was this idea of "remaining" or "abiding." In the Greek, the word *abiding* has two tenses. The first is passive. It really means to just be, to be in the present, to stay. When I looked this up, it brought a thought to my mind. I have a new Fox Red Pointing Labrador puppy, and she's gorgeous. It would be cool as a theologian to take my dog out into the field with all my hunting buddies, and when it came time to give a command, instead of the normal command of "stay," I looked at her and said, "Kelli, remain, remain." I thought that sounded more theologically correct for my dog. I never carried it through, so she responds only to "stay," but the word in John has the same meaning.

There is also an active tense to abide, and it means to "actively put ourselves in a place where we can be present with people." It's putting aside priorities and actively abiding with someone. But in either sense, here is the problem:

How do I achieve and accomplish *more* by *remaining*? How do I "abide" and become more productive? I couldn't figure out what John was trying to say. "Abiding" and "producing" seemed to be extreme opposites, and I was frustrated to get so close and yet seem to be so far from my answer.

That takes me back to my trip somewhere in northern Idaho between Kellogg and Lookout Pass. It was a beautiful October morning about 6:00 am. Not many people were on the road. The sunrise was spectacular. It was one of those sunrises where I had my iPhone out and I was trying to steer with my wrists while taking a picture out the window (come on, you've all done it). As I was driving along, despite the glorious flaming red and orange sky overhead, my spirit was perplexed. I was saying, "Lord, I just don't get it. I want to abide in you, and I want to remain in you, and I know that's got to be important, but how does that help me produce more fruit? How does remaining in you help me to have more things to show, to accomplish more goals, to get more done in my life?" I was almost in pain as I agonized over the discontinuity between these two scriptures—being a faithful worker and abiding.

I don't even know how to explain what happened next. There wasn't an audible voice, but there was a message that shot through my spirit so powerfully that I nearly drove off the road. The thought was completely foreign to anything I was thinking, and I am sure that it was the Spirit of God speaking in a loud voice directly to me. What I heard was five words that have changed my life ever since. "Scott, that's not the fruit."

I was stunned.

In those few words the Holy Spirit had created a huge vacuum in my life, in essence telling me that everything that I'd been striving for, everything that I thought was so important, everything that I thought God wanted from my life, was not the fruit that John is talking about. I wanted to cry out and say, "What do you mean that's not the fruit? I'm spending my whole life trying to produce this fruit. If that's not the fruit, what is?" But before the words got out of my mouth, right into my mind came the text from Galatians 5:22–23. "The fruit of the Spirit is love, joy, peace, patience, kindness, goodness, faithfulness, gentleness, and self control."

In one flashing moment the Spirit had replaced my drive for producing fruit with the fact that what God wanted of my life more than anything else was that I would so abide in him that everyday my life would bear the fruit of the Spirit. My world was turned upside down. I pulled off to the side of the road and sobbed. I'd been passionately pursuing the wrong fruit for forty years. I came to realize at that moment that we were not created just to *produce* fruit, we were created to *bear* fruit…and there is a world of difference between producing and bearing.

I went to the scriptures as soon as I got to my destination.

I opened up my Bible and went back to John. You know what I found? It's not about producing fruit at all! It's all about remaining, abiding, being. Eleven times in those first nineteen verses of John 15, Jesus says, "remain in me," "abide in me." The second thing I found was in, all of those places where I saw *producing* fruit, he was talking about *bearing* fruit. Seven times in these same passages, John tells us to bear fruit. It's not a text about the fruit of our own labor but about living so completely in the vine that the Holy Spirit can overwhelm our own spirits. It is in this abiding that, through us, God's Spirit touches the lives of every person we encounter with the fruit of the Spirit. It is fruit that transforms, fruit that draws all people to the vine. It is fruit that will last. We cannot produce this fruit. We can only bear it. That is our calling and our highest joy!

There is another scripture on the same theme where Paul says, "But thanks be to God who always leads us as captives in Christ's triumphal procession and uses us to spread the aroma of the knowledge of him everywhere. For we are to God the pleasing aroma of Christ among those who are being saved and those who are perishing. To the one we are an

> It is in this abiding that, through us, God's Spirit touches the lives of every person we encounter with the fruit of the Spirit. It is fruit that transforms, fruit that draws all people to the vine.

aroma that brings death, to the other an aroma that brings life" (2 Corinthians 2:14–16).

We are to smell of Christ. My friends, this is not a text calling us to go produce "Jesus perfume." This is not a command to try to figure out what Jesus smells like so we can put together a business plan, raise money, start a 501(c)3 and produce Messiah No.5. This is just another way of bearing. It is being so filled with God's Spirit that everybody who comes in contact with us smells the aroma of Christ.

My mom and dad live in Wenatchee in Central Washington. It's one of the apple capitals of the world. My dad plays golf on a brand new course that is cut right through the middle of a beautiful old apple orchard. As you can imagine, the fairways are very tight. There is precious little grass between the edge of the fairway and the apple orchard. An errant shot will almost always wind up amid the trees whose branches are laden with apples. I play the course often with my dad and, well, I spend a lot of time in the apple orchard. In the spring, all the buds are out, and the bees are humming. As you walk through the apple orchard looking for your golf ball, you smell the sweet aroma of spring. Every branch is filled with sugary sap from a deeply rooted trunk, and great clusters of pink and white flowers erupt along every inch of stem, filling the air with a perfume money cannot buy. That is our call, to be branches, filled with the sap of the Holy Spirit, and bearing the pleasing aroma of Christ.

All of this brought me back to Jesus' parable in Matthew 25 and what this means for our standing before the master on the final day. What impact does this have on what we will hear?

> What will matter to our master on the final day is solely the extent to which we remained so closely in the vine that our lives bore the fruit of the Spirit. And remember, this is not even our bearing!

Based on my new reading of John 15, I reread the story of the parable of the talents. I was absolutely astounded at what I found. Look again at Matthew 25, "His master replied, 'well done *good* and *faithful* servant.'" When I put that description next to the list of the fruit of the Spirit, guess what I found? "The fruit of the Spirit is goodness and faithfulness." What Jesus says to us on the final day is not "Well done for all of your fruit producing ways." He is commending his servants for letting the Holy Spirit so live through them that the goodness and the faithfulness of God showed through in everything that they did. What will matter to our master on the final day is solely the extent to which we remained so closely in the vine that our lives bore the fruit of the Spirit. And remember, this is not even our bearing! Apart from the vine, we can do nothing! It is solely God's work done in and through us. All we are called to do is faithfully abide.

My question for you today is, what is driving you? It's ironic that in our effort to do more for God, in our effort to be producing more fruit, we often end up cutting ourselves off from abiding in the very vine that gives us life.

I'd like you to consider a new way of looking at what it means to be a follower of Christ. How different would your life be if you woke up every morning believing that the single most important thing that God wanted from you today was to so abide in Him, to so remain in Him, that the Holy Spirit would live through you, and every life you touched would be overwhelmed by the presence of the fruit of the Spirit of God? I now believe that is exactly what God is calling us to "do" with our talents.

My friends, if we will stay as branches in that vine, there will be water in dry times for us. There will be nourishing sap in the dead of winter when everything seems lost. There will be roots that will hold us firm when the wind is blowing us all around. And there will be fruit. We can spend our lives trying to be fruitful in our own power and miss what it means to bear fruit in the power of the Spirit.

There is one thing I know for sure: the legacy that you and I will leave in our work, our institutions, for our children, and for our community will be a witness to how we lived our lives and not to what we accomplished. Nobody will come to your funeral with your stock portfolio, your strategic plan, or your annual board report. They will no longer matter. What they will talk about is how much you loved. They will remember and rejoice at your joy, your peace, and the way you were patient with others. They will talk about the kindness you showed and the goodness you exhibited. They will speak of your gentleness and faithfulness and self-control. That's your legacy. That is what you are called to live out as leaders in your institutions, as parents, as children, and as brothers and sisters in the body of Christ.

Living as disciples of Jesus Christ in this first dimension means placing as our single highest priority this simple act of abiding in the vine. From that single act of submission, surrender, and absolute dependency on the vine, we will produce fruit that brings joy to the heart of God, fruit that brings transformation in our life and the life of everyone around us…fruit that will last.

Prayer of a Recovering Fruit Producer

"Gracious Lord, I am still struggling with what all this means, but I thank you so much that you open our eyes and help guide us that we might see and understand the words that you have for us. I believe there are hearts reading these words that are so committed to the treadmill of producing fruit for you that in some way they have let slip the highest priority of their lives and have become cut off from you. I pray that you would help us understand what it means from this moment forward to abide in you in every single moment. I pray that your will would be done through us, that your Spirit would fill us and that, as we meet people throughout this day and every day, they would sense

the fruit of the Spirit flowing through our lives. Live so through us that we will smell of you in every life we touch. Let that be our greatest and highest calling as we seek to be faithful laborers in the kingdom of God. In Jesus' name, amen."

THE FRUIT

Melinda Delahoyde

"**Y**ou cannot trust me too much." I came across this sentence several years ago at the end of an address given by Andrew Murray. The subject, John 15:1–15, is Jesus' call to abide in him in all our life.

I had recently become the president of Care Net (of which I am now president emeritus), the largest affiliation organization of pregnancy centers in North America. Over 1,150 Care Net pregnancy centers with 29,000 volunteers nationwide help women facing unplanned pregnancies. I was reading Murray's wonderful book, *Absolute Surrender,* and asking myself how it is that one could truly abide in Christ and rest in him in the midst of the constant pressure of raising money, meeting deadlines, and producing results that are always weighing upon the leader of any organization.

I knew what Jesus said was true. He is the vine, I am a branch. But I was struggling. I was living in a world of outcomes and measurable results. I felt the constant pressure to perform and produce those results—"fruit." After all, I was the leader of Care Net. The ministry was *my* responsibility. My real questions were these: How does a leader who is charged with the responsibility for an organization live the abiding life that Jesus desired? How do I "bear" fruit and not constantly feel the burden of "producing" results? How do I rest and abide in Christ and let him and his life in me produce the overflowing fruit he promises? How, as a follower of Jesus, do I live out the truth of John 15?

Over the next few years, God would show me and everyone at Care Net the amazing truth of those words, "We cannot trust Him too much."

Since 2003, God has been showing us at Care Net a pathway he wanted us to follow. Since 1973, over 50 million abortions have been performed in America. Over 14 million of those abortions were performed on African American women. Abortion is the number one cause of death in the black community. In New York City alone, the abortion rate for black women is sixty percent. Over eighty percent of abortions are performed in our urban centers.

Our cities are abortion strongholds, and abortion providers are easy to find in urban communities. Yet, most pregnancy centers are located in suburban and rural communities. Transportation is often difficult for women living in the city. At Care Net, we knew we had to proactively plant pregnancy centers where the majority of abortions are performed—in our cities. Providing pregnancy center ministries in urban communities became a top priority for Care Net.

We sought the advice and wisdom of top management consultants and those who were doing ministry in the cities. They provided us with great advice: we needed to go to the churches. African American pastors are great influence in their communities. With their support and help, we could build life-affirming ministries through urban churches and plant pregnancy centers in metro communities. If we were successful, we could turn the heart of our cities back to life.

That sounded wonderful, but there was one problem. We did not know those pastors. We did not have relationships with urban pastors, nor had we built trust in the African American community. We knew that trust and building relationships would be essential. At Care Net we had brought together thousands of God's people to do this work of saving unborn lives and healing women's hearts from abortion. But, when we looked around our organization, we realized we did not have all God's people at that table. We needed to change. The worst thing we could do would be to go to the cities without building the trust we knew we would need to come alongside these leaders. We knew we could not go to the cities and simply tell black, pro-life Christians how to stop abortion. Yet the needs were so great, the numbers of abortions so horrific, and God's call to us so strong that we knew this was where God was leading Care Net.

One day we gathered our staff in our small conference room. There was nothing dramatic or eloquent about the meeting. We came together as a staff that desperately needed God's wisdom and direction. We were gathered to pray. We came as "branches," and were waiting for Jesus, our vine, to give us his direction, strength, wisdom, and power. We prayed, "Father, show us your direction, guide our paths, and let us cause no pain." We knew we were helpless to make this happen. We did not know the urban communities, and we did not know whom to call. Frankly, our prayers felt so simple and weak. We were so small, and the problem was so big. How could God ever use twenty-five people in our office in northern Virginia to do his work? My faith was not great.

Several days later, I could not get the city of Detroit out of my mind. Detroit was "no man's land." No one talked about going to Detroit. We did not know anyone in Detroit. But we knew Detroit had no pregnancy centers in the heart of the city. Could God do something in Detroit? Could we trust God that much?

Several months later, one of our staff came running down the hall. She had just gotten off the phone with a pastor in Detroit. His congregation had just moved into a beautiful and large church in the heart of metro Detroit. He had heard of Care Net, and he knew we did something with pregnancy centers. He did not know exactly what a pregnancy center was, but he knew they needed one. Could we help them start a pregnancy center in Detroit?

Yes, we could! That was the beginning of a great relationship with this pastor and his congregation. Eighteen months later a pregnancy center opened. Last year this center merged with another nearby pregnancy center.

Working with pastors and leaders in our nation's cities has been so much more than a business relationship. We have prayed and worshipped together. We have met each other's families. God has given us relationships as believers and friends. Everyone is coming together at the table to help bring life to our cities.

Over the last few years, God has brought diversity to Care Net's board and staff. We have been invited to cities to speak about building life communities. Two years ago Care Net launched the Life Ambassadors Leadership Council, bringing African American pastors, bishops, and urban leaders together to develop pro-life leadership in our urban communities. Care Net's urban website provides information and resources to pro-life leaders across the country.

I do not write this with any kind of pride or professional arrogance. We could never have accomplished these things on our own. We stand back and consider in amazement and gratitude what God has done and is doing in his people. We see Jesus working as the all-powerful, always faithful vine, giving life, direction, power, and wisdom. He has opened hearts and minds and given us a common desire to stop abortion in our cities. At Care Net we came to him and simply asked. We knew that apart from him, we could do nothing. We had nowhere else to turn.

The irony of this is that the end result of our joint efforts will be very similar to the plan consultants originally presented to Care Net. The plan is a good one. Yet, if we had begun with *our* plans, our efforts would have failed miserably. The plans we develop and the work we do to implement those plans have to be the *overflow* of God's work in us—his work as the vine. As Scott Rodin has said, our work is to *bear* not to produce fruit. At Care Net, we are just beginning to see the fruit that *God is producing*.

Of course this is only the beginning, and there is much work to be done. Are there challenges? Absolutely. Are there mistakes and misunderstandings? Yes. There are discouraging days (and weeks). Slowly, we are learning not to focus on the challenges, but to remember Jesus is the vine. We are learning to abide in him and to go back to Christ to provide the power and plans we need to press ahead. Our friends at Life International have a phrase that rings true, "Intimacy with God before impact in ministry." We abide in Christ, and he will act.

Personally, this change from producing results to bearing fruit, from overwork to overflow, this life of abiding in Christ as a leader, felt like jumping off a cliff. It is always so natural to go to the work first. After all, we are the ones to whom people turn to make the impact, turn the ship around, to fix things. I feel so much better when I am thinking, designing, engaging, and creating. I am doing something.

> There is a life that looks upon each day as a chance just to be with Christ and let him lead us through the meetings, e-mails, phone calls, and decisions. There is a way of leading that does not result in burnout, frustration, and discouragement.

But I could not get away from those words of Jesus in John 15: "apart from me you can to nothing." Christ repeats those words. They are his last message to his disciples. There is another way to do the work of ministry—a way that leads to peace and rest and lets us lay the heavy responsibilities of leadership upon Jesus. There is a life that looks upon each day as a chance just to be with Christ and let him lead us through the meetings, e-mails, phone calls, and decisions. There is a way of leading that does not result in burnout, frustration, and discouragement. I could not get away from the truth of those words, "apart from me you can do nothing."

It was not just the John 15 passage. I was reading the devotionals and journals of great missionaries and preachers. These were people who "produced" great works for God. Yet they spoke of the peril of putting Christian work first, and they understood the need for abiding in Jesus as the secret of bearing fruit.

Oh, I want this life! I want the promised peace and rest in the midst of the challenges of leadership. I want the joy of getting up each day and knowing that my God is responsible for the results and that I can rest and wait on him. I want to know that the plans, programs, and initiatives we develop flow from that abiding relationship and are not the result of my chaotic, anxiety driven striving to perform.

So, each day I am trying to begin by stepping back, closing my eyes, and opening my heart to being with Christ. I am reading more from those great saints who began their days in this spirit. I am surrendering my plans, meetings, and strategies to what Christ has for that day. I am more intentional throughout the day to remember I am the branch. I spend more time thinking about Jesus as the vine. I think more about his greatness and ability to perform and act. I remember the results are his, and I ask him to show me what this means and how that works. I feel much more like a child of God and not at all like a "leader." I know he loves me and that he wants me to bear fruit.

Can we ever trust God too much? Are the words of John 15 really true for us as leaders? Yes! I am sharing this Care

Net story to encourage you. Wherever you are, whatever challenges you are facing in life and leadership, he will be faithful. You can go to him with nothing but faith, and he will prove himself strong for you. The ministries, businesses, lives, and roles we steward do not belong to us. They belong to Christ, and he is waiting for us to come to him and rest in him as the vine. As Andrew Murray so beautifully states in *Absolute Surrender*, "Christ Jesus said: 'I am the Vine, ye are the branches.' In other words: 'I, the living One who have so completely given myself to you, am the Vine. You cannot trust me too much. I am the Almighty Worker, full of a divine life and power.' You are the branches of the Lord Jesus Christ."[3]

As I look back on this amazing example of God's faithful provision for Care Net, I realize that it was one of many ways God was leading me to a deeper understanding of the power, peace, and presence of Jesus Christ. There is always a higher purpose to our work, our lives, and our leadership.

God's purpose for us, no matter who we are, is to know Jesus and to shine him forth to a dying world. Our calling, our leadership, the organizations he has called us to steward for a time, are the vineyards and fields in which we work. *But they are only a means to an end.* That end is the transformation

---

3. Murray, Andrew. *Absolute Surrender*. (Chicago: Moody Press), p. 126.

of our hearts and minds to a life of abiding, trusting, and resting in an almighty God who will use us to show his love and power to a lost world.

> God has a life of joy and peace for us. It is the abiding life of the branch in the vine.

God has a life of joy and peace for us. It is the abiding life of the branch in the vine.

The challenges we face in ministry leadership—people, programs, resources—are meant to draw us deeper in Jesus. How long does it take for us to realize that our education, gifting, resumes, and contacts will never be enough? Our trust in ourselves—in our planning and our programs—leads to the burnout and weariness that so many of us experience. Contrast that life with the life F.B. Meyer describes in his book, *Joshua and the Land of Promise:*

It is only when we apprehend the provisions of the New Covenant, which...is full of the I wills of God, that we come into rest and peace. Not what you do, but what God will do; not your bow and spear, but his right hand and his holy arm; not the energy of your good self, but the freeness of his grace.

When you confess yourself powerless...and cast yourself helplessly on him to perform all things in and through you, realizing his ideals and fulfilling his purposes...and when you are content to work out in the strength of his Spirit what he works in, will you experience the fullness of that rest which is deep as God's.[4]

We are not supposed to gather up all our strength, our intellect, our people skills, and go forth to conquer kingdoms on earth. Jesus' plan for us is so clear. "I am the vine, you are the branches. If you remain in me and I in you, you will bear much fruit" (John 15:5).

Look at the great spiritual leaders that God raised up during the second half of the nineteenth century and early twentieth century. These were men and women who traveled across the world to share Jesus. They built orphanages, schools, hospitals, and they preached from pulpits across the globe. So many of them testify to this life of rest and abiding. It was that inner life in their hearts that brought forth the great works we know today. Hudson Taylor, Andrew Murray, Amy Carmichael, Charles Spurgeon, F.B. Meyer, E. Stanley Jones, Mrs. Henry Cowmans, Hannah Whitall Smith, George Mueller, and so many others give us a leadership "training manual" for this abiding life in Jesus—and the fruit of that life. The work follows the inner life. The "doing" follows the "being." Andrew Murray talked about this idea of being and doing in an address he gave to Christian workers.

---

4. Meyer, F.B. *Joshua and the Land of Promise* (London and Edinburgh: Marshall, Morgan and Scott, ltd.), p. 187-188.

If our life in Christ be right, all will come right. There may be the need of instruction...and training. But in the long run the greatest essential is to have the full life in Christ—in other words, to have Christ working in us, working through us...The Master has such a blessing for every one of us, and such perfect peace and rest, and such joy and strength.[5]

In another passage Murray gives reason to trust God for our lives and our work.

Let me gather up all in one sentence. 'I am the Vine, you are the branches'. I am the Divine worker, full of a divine life and power. You are the branches of the Lord. You cannot trust me too much.[6]

George Mueller, the founder of orphanages in nineteenth century England, is best known as a man who trusted God alone for all ministry resources. When he died, Mueller had handled over $8 million (and had only $800 in personal possessions at his death) and helped thousands of children through his Christian homes. But Mueller's greatest desire and the true purpose of his ministry was to leave a testimony

---

5. Murray, *Absolute Surrender.* p. 111.

6. Murray, *Absolute Surrender.* p. 126.

for future Christians: a testimony to the absolute faithfulness of God for those who live a life of abiding in him. He writes in his journals:

> The first and primary object of the work was that God would be magnified...Now if I, a poor man, simply by prayer and faith, obtained without asking any individual, the means for establishing an Orphan-House, there would be something...instrumental in strengthening the faith of the children of God,...it may be seen that God is faithful still, and hears prayer still.[7]

There are hundreds of testimonies in the devotionals and journals of great leaders of the past encouraging us to take for ourselves this life of "being" in Christ, so that he may "do" through us his works in life. The testimony streams directly from the words of Jesus and the great examples of leaders in the Bible—Moses, Joshua, Isaiah, Esther, Ruth, Paul, and others. A "great cloud of witnesses" from past generations encourage us to trust and abide.

In this age when our contemporary world is desperately in need of the love and healing of Christ, at a time when all other solutions seem ineffective and unveiled evil proliferates, could it be that God is raising up a generation of

---

7. Mueller, George. *Answers to Prayer*. (Chicago: Moody Press) p. 10.

servants and leaders who will again depend upon his strength and life to bring hope and help? The Christ-centered ministries we serve—missions, rescue missions, orphan care, pregnancy centers—are his hands and feet in the world. In whatever position or role we are called, in business or politics, as parents and pastors, it is from within our ranks that real transformation and change will come to our world.

> In this age when our contemporary world is desperately in need of the love and healing of Christ, at a time when all other solutions seem ineffective and unveiled evil proliferates, could it be that God is raising up a generation of servants and leaders who will again depend upon his strength and life to bring hope and help?

But transformation will first come to our hearts. The abiding life always leads to a life of power and strength and service. My prayer is for his revival in our hearts.

I pray for myself and all of us that he will pierce our hearts. I ask myself if I will surrender my agenda, my plans, my gifts, my fears, my will—my life—so that Christ would live through me. I ask myself if I will surrender to a life of abiding in Christ, if I will surrender to be a branch. His great love beckons me to say yes.

BREADTH

THE SECOND DIMENSION

SET FREE TO LIVE

R. Scott Rodin

" *Now the Lord is the Spirit, and where the Spirit of the Lord is, there is freedom, and we all who with unveiled faces contemplate the Lord's glory are being transformed into his image with ever increasing glory which comes from the Lord who is the Spirit"* (2 Corinthians 3:17).

"For we know that our old self was crucified with him so that the body ruled by sin might be done away with, that we should no longer be slaves to sin because anyone who has died has been set free from sin." (Romans 6:6-7)

The common theme in these two texts is freedom. In Romans Paul speaks of being freed from slavery. How do we relate to this idea? If you are like me, you have never been an actual slave to anyone. The problem with freedom is that it only has value if we understand ourselves first to be in bondage, in a real slavery that robs us of our freedom. Without that understanding, talk of freedom is meaningless. So how are we supposed to understand what Paul is saying?

What is the slavery from which you and I are being called in Christ to be set free?

The short answer is that Paul is talking about sin. Paul likens sin to a heavy yoke that is worn by a slave. It is meant to be a graphic illustration of a punishing bondage and absolute enslavement. Our challenge in reading this is that in our current culture sin has lost most all of its terrifying and devastating character. A modern day metaphor may be that we tend to treat the sin in our lives more like a fly on the potato salad than a rattlesnake in the living room. Did you catch that? Flies on the potato salad at the summer picnic are annoying. You shoo them away and hope they leave and don't return, but they just keep coming back. And after a while you pretty much ignore them. It's not such a big deal.

Not so if you came home and found a rattlesnake in your living room. You wouldn't say, "Oh, kids, just walk around the snake. If you give him a little room, you'll get used to him. Just ignore him. He will go away after a while, so let's just pretend he's not even there." Not likely! If you found a rattlesnake in your living room, it would get your full attention. You would treat it as a mortal enemy and do everything possible as fast as possible to get rid of it. It is a threat to your very life…*and so is the sin in your life*. Perhaps now we can better understand Paul's admonition that if we don't deal with our sin, if we ignore it or patronize it or minimize it and just hope it will go away, it will become to us a heavy yoke of absolute slavery.

The yoke that weighs us down from sin comes in many forms. Fear, anxiety, and worry are yokes of slavery. Discouragement as well as pride can be yokes of slavery, as can envy, bitterness, failure to forgive, cynicism, and jealousy. Going back to the first dimension, the sin that weighs us down is everything that keeps you and me from daily abiding in the vine. It exists in our lives as compromise, selfishness, and a lack of trust, among many other names. If we allow sin to continue in our lives, we are constantly having that yoke put upon us.

> Our enemy's intent is to so burden us down under the collective weight of our own compromises that we are rendered ineffective.

All of us are struggling under some yoke of slavery, and the enemy uses this to his advantage. Our enemy's intent is to so burden us down under the collective weight of our own compromises that we are rendered ineffective. Let me explain. When the enemy looks out at the people of God, he knows it's not likely that he is going to be able to steal our faith from us or get us to reject Christ as our savior. We are secure in the hands of God. So, if the enemy can't make us unfaithful, he will happily settle for making us ineffective. He will work to neutralize us as faithful and effective workers in the kingdom of God. He does so by enticing us to place on ourselves the yoke of slavery to sin. And he specifically targets those areas of our lives that rob us of peace, steal our joy and render us impotent.

Christ came to rescue us from this peaceless, joyless, power-less, and ultimately empty life. He came to take off the yokes we bear, set us free from slavery to sin, and send us off on a completely new journey as his beloved children.

One-Kingdom Freedom

There's another way of looking at the freedom Christ won for us. It comes from the end of Matthew 6:31–34:

> So do not worry saying what shall we eat, what shall we drink, what shall we wear, for pagans run after all these things, but your heavenly Father knows that you need them, but seek first his kingdom and his righteous-ness and all these things will be given to you as well. Therefore don't worry about tomorrow, for tomorrow will worry about itself. Each day has enough trouble of its own.

Jesus admonishes us to seek first the kingdom of God. Have you ever wondered what other kingdom we might choose to seek instead? If Jesus was so emphatic about seek-ing first the kingdom of God, what did he understand to be the alternative? I believe the kingdom that competes for our allegiance is the kingdom you and I try to build for our self. In our sinful nature, all of us are personal kingdom builders. We spend our lives constructing the walls and boundaries of what we value in this world and place within them those things that we seek to control. Everything over which we proclaim to be owners is what constitutes the contents of our little, separate, second kingdom. Amazingly, as people of faith, we build our kingdoms right alongside the kingdom of God. The stuff in our kingdom consist of everything over which we like to play the lord.

The first step to embracing the freedom that Christ won for us, the freedom that leads to life abundant, is to acknowledge that we are second kingdom builders. The second step is to name those things that exist in our kingdom. We must confess, "I am living like I own this myself. I've climbed upon my throne, put a little crown on my head, and said 'this is mine.'" In our kingdoms, we will experience the yoke of slavery because fear and anxiety and frustration and discouragement are attached like parasites to everything we call "ours."

In the end, either the totality of our life is submitted to God's lordship or we attempt to seize a counterfeit control and a competing lordship for ourselves. Both decisions have consequences.

The One Gift We All Want
Let's come at this in a different way. Imagine I place in front of you an ornately decorated wooden box that was made to hold an item of immense value. I tell you that in this box is

an object that kings and rulers across the ages have waged war in order to obtain. The wealthiest and most powerful people in our society amass all the wealth they possibly can, hoping and praying that one day they may be able to take hold of what's in this box. And every single person reading this book, including you, would give everything they owned in order to possess what is in this box. Intrigued?

When the box is opened, what is found is a simple wooden stick that resembles a magic wand. With it is a set of instructions that read as follows:

The bearer of this wand is empowered to control all of the people, all of the circumstances, and all of the outcomes in his or her life. Just wave this wand and:

- *Flat tires will happen for people who cut you off in traffic.*
- *No one sitting near you on an airplane will ever cough or sneeze and there will be no children within ten rows.*
- *Dogs and cats will obey your every word.*
- *Children will ask for and actually take your advice.*
- *You can replace every frustrating, inactive, or overly critical coworker, boss, or board member with ones who love everything you do.*
- *Troublesome employees will choose to leave and thank you for the opportunity to serve.*
- *Every new program or idea that you present will*

be joyfully embraced and accepted by your entire organization.

- *Every customer will buy, donors will say yes, and grantors will be delighted to receive every application you send them.*
- *Everyone will always give you the full benefit of the doubt for every decision that you ever make.*

This wand gives you total control of your life. Wave this wand and the pain in your life will go away. Wave this wand and your inner sense of inadequacy will quit haunting you. Wave this wand and your addiction will finally end, your doubts and discouragements will fade away, you will make all of the money you need, and you will find the joy and meaning in life you so desperately crave. All you have to do is wave the wand.

Pretty cool, huh? Of course, such a wand does not exist, but the problem is we pretend that it does. As second kingdom builders, we seek to claim this wand for ourselves. We spend our lives trying to control the people around us and the circumstances we encounter, believing that if we just had more control our lives can be happier, more meaningful, and less painful. Then we can finally experience some happiness and joy.

The sad secret is that, even though we pretend that we have a lot of control, in the end we know we really don't. In fact, the more we try to control things around us, the more we realize that life tends to control us. What results is an "if only" kind of existence. "*If only* I could get my spouse to…. *If only* I could just make more money…. *If only* I could get the people I work with to be more…. *If only* my church would, my pastor would, my boss would…." Finish these sentences for yourself, and add additional ones that are true for you. In this controlling mindset, as we sit frantically waving our wand over the stuff and people in our own kingdoms from the seat of our own little throne, the joy and peace we so desperately yearn for will forever remain just an "if only" away.

Naming the Battle

This is the battle of our lives…and it is a battle for lordship. The stakes in this battle are greatly increased when we are called to lead. Simply put, it is a battle between whether our leadership is going to be dominated by ownership and control or the freedom of the steward-leader. The stakes for this decision could not be higher.

As leaders, we now fight this battle with and on behalf of others. For the people we lead and the organizations we serve, everything depends on whether we choose to be owner-leaders or steward-leaders.

As stewards, we understand that all of life is on loan, and we respond by living lightly in this world as caretakers of that which is not ours. This results in a life of real freedom to which we respond with joyful obedience. These are the marks of the victorious steward: freedom, obedience, and joy. At battle with this freedom is an enemy who seeks to steal our joy by luring us into playing the owner. As owners, we claim to have control over our time, talents, and resources that we can employ for our own good and gain. Once we shift our perspective from steward to owner, we experience the loss of the carefree and become enslaved to the neverending work of maintaining our control and gaining more of it.

Owner-leaders take their organization on their own shoulders and tie their own self-worth to its success, which requires that they protect turf, use people to accomplish their own purposes, and exert control over every situation. Their leadership is typified by power and fear, and it results in anxiety, stress, and burnout. If your self-worth is tied to your success, you will "own" your job. Leaders who own their jobs will view the people around them as the means to the achievements they so desperately must attain. They will eventually justify every means to succeed because their self-worth is bound up with the tangible outcomes of their work performance. They can't afford to fail. As a result, owner-leaders seize control and lead by fiat. Their use of power and fear may come about even against their own desires to do so. Unwittingly, they develop the kind of authoritarian traits that they despise in others. Owner-leaders are not only in bondage themselves, but they will enslave the people that they lead.

If you have ever worked for a real owner-leader, you know the devastating impact it has on team morale and personal effectiveness. Ironically, organizational failure most often results from the kind of leadership that is most driven to succeed. Owner-leaders ultimately destroy organizations and the people who serve there. Do you have an owner-leader in your life? Do you see one in the mirror?

> Owner-leaders ultimately destroy organizations and the people who serve there.

The alternative choice is the life of the steward-leader. Steward-leaders who have been set free by the power of God seek obedience above every other motivation in life. They are not driven by the need to prop up their reputation or undergird their self-worth, but simply by hearing the word of God and being obedient. They do so because position, power, praise, and plaudits no longer carry any allure. They are stewards, and their sole heart's desire is to do the will of the owner. They can look out across all that is in front of them and declare, "It is not mine. I've been set free. I'm called to joyfully steward all that I see."

As a result, steward-leaders give away power. They promote others and are comfortable when other people receive more acclaim than they do. Steward-leaders build people up and allow others to shine. They are not threatened by the people around them getting the credit, and they make sure God always gets the glory because it is not about them. Ultimately, steward-leaders who are free can be used by God to set their people free.

Steward-leaders are also not manipulated by their circumstances. They are at peace in struggle or in success because the battle belongs to the Lord. It's God's fight, God's organization, and ultimately God will prevail.

Can you say to yourself with conviction, "It's God's job, not my job. These are God's people, not my people. We are supported by God's givers, not my donors. It's God's board, not my board. It all belongs to him, and if it all belongs to him, then whether he gives us plenty or whether he puts us through a time of struggle, I can be at peace because he simply calls me to be a faithful steward and trust him for the rest"?

Steward leaders yield their organization to God in this way and seek only to be obedient, responsive servants of the true owner. As a result, they are set free to lead! As Christians who are called to lead, we are on a journey from our old ownership ways to the victorious life of the steward-leader. The journey is marked by an almost continuous battle to let God to be the absolute Lord of our life, and of all aspects of our calling as leaders.

Claiming the Freedom

How are you faring in this battle? Where are you on this journey? The answers may be best found by asking your staff, your peers, your children, and your spouse. What would they say about your progress on this journey? Will you ask them? They will remind you that the real evidence as to our steward/owner orientation lies far more in how we live and lead than by what we accomplish. This world is desperately in need of faithful, joyful stewards who have sold out completely to Jesus Christ, who stake no claims for themselves, but who rejoice in the success of everyone around them—stewards who are genuinely free!

> If you want to be set free by the Spirit of God, you must be willing to name the second kingdoms in your life.

I believe today that each one of us is called into the life of a faithful steward. My questions to you are simply these: Do you want to be free? Do you want to set aside all of your ownership struggles, lay aside everything that calls you to control the people and the things around you, and know that sweet freedom of a steward of God? If you do, then I want to invite you into the freedom Christ has for you this very minute.

The journey to freedom starts by confessing your own kingdom-building ways. Name the things in your life where you wave that wand with all of your might and desperately grasp at control. Right now, lay those things before God. Name those things in your life that you hold on to and make a commitment right now to let them go. If you want to be set free by the Spirit of God, you must be willing to name the second kingdoms in your life.

Once you've named them in you heart, create a picture in your mind where you can actually see and feel what it is like to take off your heavy crown, step off that throne, and willingly and joyfully lay it down at the feet of Jesus. Then just walk away.

The journey to freedom is empowered each day with a simple prayer, "Lord, it is not mine, it is yours...*all of it!*" Pray it every morning before you leave your bed, and don't get up until you know in your spirit that sweet sense of freedom that comes as a gift from the Holy Spirit into the heart of a steward-leader who is set free to lead. Say it out loud to yourself over and over again: "It is not mine; it's yours—all of it. Now come, Lord Jesus, and set me free."

The Prayer of Freedom

"Gracious Lord, in this moment, whatever bondage I am under, whatever sin or discouragement or fear or frustration I am experiencing that comes from holding on so tight, I lay it down and give it back to you. And now, Lord, by the great and awesome power of your Holy Spirit, fill me, free me, take this yoke from my shoulders. Let me hear the sound of shackles falling to the floor, for I am no longer bound by the yoke of slavery. I am no longer grasping to hold on to my wand, claiming my place on my own throne, but Lord I give it all to you. It is yours. Fill

me with a newfound freedom that I may see every part of my life through the eyes of a steward. Create in me a heart that wants only to be faithful and obedient to you. Thank you Lord, that you came to set us free, and remind me every day that as the Son sets me free, I will be free indeed. In the name of our risen, liberating, powerful Lord and savior, Jesus Christ, amen."

THE FREEDOM

William F. High

I don't tell this story very often. It's a story of my failure, and who likes to tell those stories? But maybe it's a story of my success, too. You can be the judge.

I grew up poor—dirt poor, as I like to say. My father was the oldest of eight children who grew up in a three-room log cabin. They were hillbillies tucked away at the bottom of a dead-end holler at the foot of the Ozark Mountains. For them, going out to hunt meant the difference of a stocked pot or slim pickings.

I was named after my great grandfather, William, who I never met. He was a deadeye with a rifle, as legend has it. And he was poor, too. So by the time my father was born, our socioeconomic status was pretty well locked in, and my dad was destined for a life of poverty. His options for his future were limited: pick up another Ozark homestead and become a rock farmer or join the military.

He joined the military. His travels led him to Japan, where he met my mother. They promptly got busy having children, and pretty soon there were six kids running around. I was the fifth.

I don't think I realized we were poor until I was about five years old. I'd gone to collect the mail and the mailman made a disparaging remark about my hand-me-down jeans, shirt, and coat that didn't fit. My dad left the service, and times were tough for a blue-collar guy who drank a little too much. So we found ourselves on welfare, and I remember riding in the back of a pickup truck on top of cans of welfare cheese, corn, and spam, courtesy of the US government.

Growing up poor did something to me. It made me want something—something more than I had. My dad died when I was just twelve. Cancer took him before the alcoholism did. My mom was left with nothing. She'd barely worked outside the home, had no driver's license and no life insurance, and still had six kids to raise. She lamented that my dad had never been willing to own a house.

This experience produced a seed in my twelve-year-old mind. I wanted to own something and to have a place we called our own so we were not just vagabonds and nomads.

An interlude is necessary here. At the same time my father was dying, a little country church was getting started. A family down the street from us brought us a children's Bible storybook. I devoured it and became enthralled with the stories of Noah, Abraham, Moses, Joshua, Joseph, and Jesus. Through the persistent prayers of others, the Word of

God, and faithfulness of a few families, I came to know the person of Christ.

That grounding in God's Word saved me from so much of the heartache of junior and senior high. Soon virtually every member of our family had come to know Christ. God's saving grace in my life was but one part of a work that was still to come.

Fast-forward a number of years. The seeds that had been planted in our family bore fruit. Each of my older siblings had a drive to succeed and to achieve. Like them, I found myself in college and ultimately law school. Each of these steps was a miracle from the Lord. Only He could have made it possible for a poor kid from the Ozarks to afford higher education.

After law school, I was offered a position in one of the most prestigious law firms in a major US city. It was quite a culture shock. For the first time, I was surrounded by men and women who knew what money meant, what to spend it on, and how to look good. There were silk ties, expensive suits, and even more expensive cars.

I felt out of place, but nonetheless, there was something I could understand: ownership. The partners in the firm dangled the carrot of ownership in the firm. They called it "becoming partner." With partnership, you got a share in the firm, a percentage of the profits, and a right to vote.

The idea of becoming an owner was a huge deal to me. It was everything I did not have growing up. I thought ownership would produce purpose, a place to belong, and provision for my family.

So I chased the carrot. I was often one of the first ones in the building except for one fanatic senior partner. He saw me there in the early morning hours and took an interest in me. He gave me some work to do, which gave me the opportunity to work alongside him. Sometimes it meant really late hours.

I took on big caseloads and became one of the leaders in the billable hour category. I bought the suits, the ties, the shoes, and although I could never really afford the fancy car, I thought all that would come…someday. My mom crowed with pride—her son the lawyer—and I basked in the glow as well.

The seven-year partnership track was long and hard. During those years, my wife and I had four little kids—two girls and two boys. And they all wanted attention. But I'd always heard it said that the law is a jealous mistress. It also wanted my attention. So I pressed on until two fateful events occurred.

As I was nearing the end of my associate tenure, I was expecting to be called into my senior partner's office and be rewarded with the fruits of my labor. However, something much different happened. On a car trip to visit a client, the senior partner opened a conversation with, "Let's talk about partnership." From there he explained that the firm had voted to *not* make me a partner.

I don't remember much of the conversation from there. It was a blurry mess. He told me that the decision was "deferred" and that I could still make partner. But my world was rocked.

In the coming months, I felt a variety of emotions: anger, shame, humiliation, but mostly confusion. I thought I was chasing ownership and purpose. It had all been yanked away. And I felt fear, too—what if they took away my position totally? How would I provide for my family?

In the coming months, I felt a variety of emotions: anger, shame, humiliation, but mostly confusion. I thought I was chasing ownership and purpose. It had all been yanked away.

But most of all, it was the questions that came. Just what was my purpose? What was I chasing? What was my aim? Was it really ownership, a share in the firm? And to what end? I began looking for other jobs, mainly out of fear. I even considered a total career change. I did career assessments. I searched the Scriptures, and I prayed. In it all, the Lord was very quiet.

Finally, during the midst of this crazy, hazy storm-filled time, the second catalytic event occurred. I'd been travelling a lot, which meant missing a lot of evenings at home. It was on one of those nights where I slipped into bed late, and my wife (my ever patient Brooke) whispered, "You need to go talk to Ashley [our oldest]. She needs you."

I groaned, but I slipped out of bed and padded to her room. I shook her awake and held her. Inexplicably, she cried. At first, no words came. Finally, I asked her what was wrong. In her five-year-old wisdom, she told me flat out, "Daddy, you've been gone too much."

After calming her and comforting her, I retreated to our living room no longer sleepy. There in the darkness with the tears of my daughter still fresh on my shoulder, the Lord spoke to me from Psalms 127:2:

> It is in vain that you rise up early
> and go late to rest,
> eating the bread of anxious toil;
> for he gives to his beloved sleep.

When I heard those words, I burst out laughing—at myself. The Lord was trying to show me how foolish I'd been. At that moment, I realized how futile my efforts really were. I realized it was all vanity. I had been striving, getting up early, going to bed late, and yet the Lord desired to love me and give me sleep.

And so with very little fanfare, I let go of my desire to own something. I set aside my lifelong drive to be an owner.

The succeeding months were a great adventure. I began to concentrate on what was sure in my life: the certainty of heaven and the place Jesus had provided for me. I found myself going to work with this crazy smile on my face. People came up to me and asked me, "What's wrong with you?"

When I let go of my desire to become an owner, I experienced this marvelous freedom. I wasn't worried. I was freed to do what God had called me to do.

I saw my place in the firm differently. I saw God had put me there to minister. I realized I was a steward of relationships. I saw God had put a whole group of people around me who needed me to be their Jesus. I was their shepherd, and they were my flock.

I was elevated to manage the paralegals in our office. And because of my own "failure," other lawyers started coming to me for advice. I was able to lead a Bible study there. Even outside the firm, volunteer opportunities opened up for me to minister in the city.

Gradually, slowly, the Lord unlocked the grip of ownership from me and allowed me to move to a place where I just became His minister, His steward, and His manager right where I was.

As those chains fell, it became clear the Lord was leading me away from the law firm toward a position of ministry. It was not clear exactly what that position would be, but I could feel the tug. So did my wife, and so did others around me.

Even as I was being led away from the firm, another strange twist of events occurred. The same law firm that had turned me down for partnership came back to me and offered me "ownership" in the firm. I laughed.

My wife and I considered turning down the ownership offer. Now that it was in front of us, we found it didn't mean anything anymore. It was far more exciting to be a steward and leave the ownership up to God. It's all His anyway.

So here's the final puzzle piece. I did in fact become an owner in the firm. But I also did in fact leave the firm to join a ministry.

Today, I'm the Chief Executive Officer of the National Christian Foundation *Heartland* (NCF). We are the largest public Christian foundation in the country, and we work with over ten thousand donors around the country. Our mission? To teach people how to be wise stewards and give away their ownership. Giving away that ownership means tangibly giving away things like cars, trucks, boats, real estate, and even ownership interests in companies. It usually takes spiritual transformation before it becomes a financial transaction.

The work has grown so large that we've started another entity called iDonate.com that allows people to give away tangible items online. We've also started an entity called Generous Life that encourages families to think generationally in their giving—to transfer not only their wealth, but also their values to successive generations, even down to the seventh generation. The greatest failure we see families make is the failure to think generationally.

It's God's sense of humor that led me to where I am today. My friend Mart Green always tells me that your deepest wound is typically your greatest point of ministry. The roots of ownership are difficult things to extract.

> Your deepest wound is typically your greatest point of ministry. The roots of ownership are difficult things to extract.

And the extraction process is ongoing. Even today I wrestle with these issues. The ownership issues arise with my cars, my house, my toys, my time. It is easy to demand my way with those things—because that's what owners do. Similarly, as I've been part of starting new companies, the same desires for shares, ownership, and control all arise.

As I face those old temptations, I find I can only eradicate the roots by careful self-examination. The more I assess my desires through the lens of God's Word, the more likely I will see myself accurately. I need people around me as well—people motivated by the same desires: to live simply, give generously, and experience freedom. Indeed, the greatest antidote for ownership greed is abundant generosity. The more I give, the less I'm inclined to hold on to the things of this world.

Many reading this book will find themselves wrestling with the same relentless drive to be an owner. I'd encourage you to examine why, but particularly to conduct that examination in light of all of eternity. We all know we can take nothing from this planet. We will all stand before Jesus empty-handed. On judgment day, He'll simply ask us about our stewardship: how did we manage what He gave us—not what we owned. This perspective can keep us forever fresh. It's a great adventure—this journey from ownership to stewardship—and it's my hope that more will come join me day by day.

Depth

The Third Dimension

MEANS AND ENDS

R. Scott Rodin

We have been proposing that the true life of a disciple of Jesus Christ is lived in three dimensions. These three dimensions give our life the height, breadth, and depth that result in a vibrant, abundant life. We were created and redeemed to live lives of spiritual vitality, lives that draw people, lives that breathe life into people, and lives that inspire people. Yet too often we let the busyness, the challenges, the worries, the fears, and the frustrations we face cause our spiritual lives to become flat, two-dimensional, or maybe even one-dimensional.

Let's look at the third dimension of the life of a disciple. The primary text for this third dimension comes from Matthew 22:37–40. Jesus is replying here to the Pharisees who are asking him, "What is the greatest commandment?" This is what he says:

> Love the Lord your God with all your heart and with all your soul and with all your mind. This is the

first and greatest commandment." The second is like it. "Love your neighbor as yourself." All the law and the prophets hang on these two commandments.

Jesus' response helps tie some things together. I want us to see that this third dimension, this idea of loving our neighbors as we love ourselves, can only happen as a result of the first two dimensions. This progression and inner-relationship is critical for us to understand.

In the first dimension, we defined what it meant to be fruit producers. We are tempted to spend our lives believing that we are called to produce fruit, that the abundant life is all about production, about getting things done, accomplishing tasks, and achieving measurable goals. If that's the single thing that drives us, it will impact the relationships that we have around us.

You see, if all I care about is producing, then you, my brothers and sisters in Christ, become a means of production. My relationship with you will have one primary focus—helping me achieve what I need to achieve in life. This perspective colors significantly the way in which we interact with others. We may desire to love our neighbor as Christ commands, but we will not escape the temptation to see them as means to an end.

When, however, we submit ourselves fully to be branches and accept the truth that God calls us not to produce fruit but to bear fruit, the Holy Spirit flows through us with unimaginable power and grace. When that work of the Spirit seeps into our souls, our relationships with the people around us change. When I desire to bear fruit, I yield myself to the work of touching the lives of the people around me. Discipleship in this first dimension convicts me that I cannot love my neighbor and be a fruit producer in this world.

The second dimension is much the same. If we are owner-leaders, we will believe that we own our relationships and our organizations, and as a result, we will live and lead through controlling everyone around us. We cannot love our neighbor and control them at the same time. We can't seek to manipulate others for our own success and love them the way Christ calls us to love them. When it comes to leadership, the owner-leader who is driven to produce will wreak havoc on his or her organization. Have you ever worked for someone who is bent on producing, getting bottom line results—someone who owns their organization, who ties their reputation to the success of the organization that they lead? If you have, then you know that they tear organizations apart. You may find some of this in your own life as you seek to lead others. Ask yourself, "To what degree am I driven to produce? To what degree do I own my organization?" It's a word of warning for us as we think truly about what it means to love the people around us.

As we move now to this third dimension, here is the image that I want to put in front of you.

What does it mean to love our neighbor? This has been a significant transformational image for me in my life. It has changed the way I think about every person I encounter, everyone with whom I interact. It reminds me that every person on this earth is on a journey of faith and faithfulness with God. Every person, believer and non-believer alike, is on such a journey. God is calling, wooing, encouraging, and transforming us on that journey. None of us live in an isolated moment. God desires that we all become transformed into the image of Christ. God is at work in every life, every minute of every day, and anytime that I interact with another person, I enter into their journey. It may be for the briefest of moments: talking to the cashier at the grocery store or the person sitting next to me on a plane. Or it may be more substantial interactions with family and friends, coworkers and fellow church members.

Whatever the duration or intensity of the interaction, I become a part of their journey. The question is, will I yield myself to be used by God to help them in whatever work he is doing in them as part of their greater journey, or will I consider them in the static moment that marks our intersection? When I ask myself that question, it changes the way that I interact with people. Simply put, do I engage with the people God puts in my path in isolated moments or do I value them as co-travelers on a journey of transformation?

Let's look at Luke 18:35–43 as one example:

As Jesus approached Jericho, a blind man was sitting by the roadside begging. Get the image in your mind. When he heard the crowd going by, he asked what was happening. They told him, "Jesus of Nazareth is passing by." And he called out, "Jesus, son of David, have mercy on me!" Now those who led the way rebuked him and said to him to be quiet. But he shouted all the more, "Son of David, have mercy on me!" Jesus stopped, and he ordered the man to be brought to him. When he came near, Jesus asked him, "What do you want me to do for you?" "Lord, I want to see," he replied. Jesus said to him, "Receive your sight. Your faith has healed you." Immediately he received his sight and followed Jesus, praising God. When all the people saw it, they also praised God.

This is a perfect illustration of our point. The disciples and followers of Jesus, those who supposedly knew him most intimately, were leading this procession, trying to get Jesus from one place to another. They were on a mission. They were producing fruit. They had to keep moving. They didn't have time for Jesus to stop and chat. So when they heard this man start shouting out, they considered him an obstacle, an annoyance to be ignored or silenced. The disciples saw this man in a static moment. When Jesus saw this man, I believe he considered him in the context of his life's journey. He saw him at his birth, when he came out of his mother's womb blind. He saw him as a child never being able to do what the other kids could do. He saw a young man's dreams of marriage and family dashed. And he saw the day that he became committed to the hopeless life of sitting by the side of the road begging. Jesus saw his heart breaking, saw his dreams dashed, saw his future taken away from him. And into this man's lifelong journey had come this one momentary encounter with the great healer, the King of Kings, and Lord of Lords. Seeing him in his journey, Jesus stopped. He healed him. He changed his life.

We see the same "journey mindset" when Samuel comes to anoint David as king. God speaks these words to the prophet in 1 Samuel 16:7: "Don't consider his appearance or his height, [talking about one of the other sons] for I have rejected him. The Lord does not look at the things people look at. People look at the outward appearance, but the Lord looks at the heart."

As God's people, what do we look at when we see the people that are around us? We are called to be Christ-followers, to intersect the lives of the people around us as co-journeyers, fellow travelers on this road of reconciliation and restoration. We are all in this process of transformation, and we are called to help one another and to be used by God to bless one another on that journey. So

> We are all in this process of transformation, and we are called to help one another and to be used by God to bless one another on that journey.

here's the question: how do you think people experience you in the relationships that you have? If I were to talk to your friends, your brothers and sisters, your coworkers, your parents, your spouses, your children, what kind of relationships would you be known for?

Scripture tells us we are stewards of these relationships. My attitude changed dramatically when I realized that God just might be calling me to bring a blessing into the lives of the people I touch. This is not easy. There are people who I just want to write off, and others who tempt me to practice creative avoidance rather than engage them. In my life, there is one particular person who just drives me nuts. Every time I'm around him, which isn't very often, I come away feeling lousy. He has the ability in a thirty-second conversation to leave you shaking your head and wondering why you even try. He's divisive. He's spiteful. He's a person whom I cannot help but see in a static moment. As I'm writing this page, I realize that never one time in any of my encounters with him have I ever asked God, "How can I be a blessing in the journey that you have this person on?" I've never seen him as on a journey, only as an annoyance. How can I be the hands and feet of Christ with such an attitude? How do I become part

> Until I am willing to embrace him as a fellow traveler and understand that I'm on the same journey with him, I will never serve him as my neighbor like Christ commanded.

of his journey and perhaps have a word for him that God would put on my heart? I can't. Until I am willing to embrace him as a fellow traveler and understand that I'm on the same journey with him, I will never serve him as my neighbor like Christ commanded. Even worse, I will never open myself up to the possibility that maybe he has a word for me on my journey.

When we allow Christ to open our eyes and see people as he sees them, everything around us changes. We see the people in grocery store lines differently. The people with twenty items in a fifteen-item line no longer arouse our wrath. Instead we are willing to consider that maybe God put them in front of us so that we might be able to enter into that person's journey and help them along the way.

Leadership in this third dimension is all about vision. It's about changing the way in which we look at one another. You're going to bump into people today. There are people sitting next to you in a waiting room or standing in front of you at the bank that need to hear a word from you today. There are people who come in and out of your life desperately needing in their journey people to speak into their lives. If you bump into them and are frustrated because they got on the elevator before you instead of taking a moment to learn about their journey and blessing them on that way, you've missed an opportunity. Don't we all need those people in our lives? Don't we need people who are willing to enter in to our journeys and bless us? Let's do that for one another.

Here is the challenge. Pray each day for eyes to see your neighbor as God sees them. Develop the heart of a fellow traveler and pray for the freedom to be used by God to bless them on that journey. "Bless us Lord, that we may be able to be a blessing." This prayer requires new eyesight. It requires that we be free as faithful stewards. Owners can't pray that prayer. I can't both look at you as someone that I need as a means to my own end and care about your journey. If I am to love you as Christ calls me to love, I must see my relationship with you as an end in itself. I have to love you for who you are, just as God called me to do. It requires the presence of the Holy Spirit in my life. I'll tell you real honestly, I can't do this on my own. If I don't have the Holy Spirit working in and through me, I will slip back into that old mentality. People will just bug me and bother me and be in my way until the Spirit gets my attention and reminds me what I'm called to do as I journey through this life.

What would it require for you to become the kind of person that lifted people up around you, that empowered people around you and allowed the fruit of the Spirit to live through your life? Life in all three dimensions means submission to Jesus Christ like branches submitted to a vine. It means giving up our thrones and knowing the absolute freedom that we have as stewards of all parts of our lives. It means entering with love into the journeys of the people that are around us so that we may be co-journeyers, co-travelers, that we might bring blessing into the lives of the people around us. That kind of equipping can only come from the Holy Spirit working in you.

Prayer for the Journey

"Dear Lord, open my eyes that I may see the people you place around me as you see them. Give me a love for my neighbor that reflects your love for me. Drive from me the need to use others for my own advancement. Overwhelm my agenda with your vision

for my place in the lives of those with whom you surround me. And let me really love them, serve them, and be present in their lives as a witness to you. Help me to so completely lose myself in submission to you that I may fully find myself in service to others. In the name of the lover of my soul, Jesus Christ my Lord, amen."

THE JOURNEY

Pat McCown

In the J. R. R. Tolkien classic, *The Hobbit,* Gandalf the wizard solicits an unassuming and cautious hobbit, Bilbo Baggins, to embark on a monumental journey of a lifetime. The only certainty that Gandalf could give Bilbo about his adventures was that he "would never be the same." That journey changed the very core of Bilbo's existence. So it is with us. We barely recognize the fact that we are all on a transformational, radical, never-be-the-same journey in our own lives. We are all travelers on the road God has set us upon, and I am certain none of us will be the same at the end.

My personal journey began long before I became a follower of Jesus. I didn't even recognize I was on a journey. I was blind to the reality that everyone around me was a fellow sojourner. Marty was a boyhood friend who was on his own personal quest toward Christ. Marty and I had not talked very much since graduating from high school, but the intersection of our paths was about to change my life.

One Sunday afternoon while we rode motorcycles, Marty challenged me by bringing forward some questions regarding my faith, or lack thereof. Although I had gone to church all my life with my parents, I really had little if any relationship with Jesus. Marty awakened my heart with questions, none of which I could answer with any certainty. Even though my encounter with Marty was brief, I could see, taste, and feel that Marty's life and heart were being transformed by God. I was the benefactor of Marty's journey, and that intersection caused a change that had eternal consequences.

Things started changing in me as I began to yield my life to the lover of my soul. It seemed that as I began to plug into the vine, new thoughts, visions, and energy started coming into my relationships. I began to consider that my encounter with friends who appeared to be far from any relationship with Jesus were really opportunities to serve them, to be a kind of a road sign for their journey. Engaging in conversation about my faith with friends became a more relaxed and natural part of my life. I can look back now and appreciate that through these encounters the fruits of the Holy Spirit were being manifested for the benefit of others.

My journey soon took on greater direction and purpose. I began to see new goals for my path. What was even more real to me was that everyone else around me was somewhere along a pathway as well. I was slowly moving away from wanting to be liked by others at any cost to helping others in their personal journey to fall in love with Jesus. I was being changed into a disciple as a result of intersecting the lives of others.

For several summers, I worked as a college student with a house painting company. Our crew consisted of several college-aged students, and we had a lot of fun working together. I can't remember anything specific happening regarding my faith journey during those summers, but some twenty years later I ran into one of the guys that I worked with during my house painting days. I didn't even recognize him. To my surprise, he joyfully announced that he had given his life to Jesus about fifteen years after we had last worked together. I was stunned. He went on to tell me of the impact of the conversations we had during our summers together. I couldn't even remember those conversations, but the intersections of our journeys had somehow pointed the way to Jesus for him.

In 1 Corinthians 3:6, Paul tells us that while one plants and another waters, it is God who makes things grow. So it is with people we encounter along our journey. Knowingly or not, we may plant a seed in someone's life, or water the seed someone else already planted. And perhaps if we allow the Lord to bear his fruit in our lives, others may taste and see that the Lord is good.

As Scott and Melinda have shared with you, John 15 talks about our need to abide in the vine. In a perfect world we are *constantly abiding* in the vine, becoming a conduit of

God's grace. In the real world, I believe we are *learning to abide*. As we do, we begin bearing fruit for his glory and allowing others to taste that fruit within us. Ideally we only go forward down our path; there is no diversion and certainly no reverse. But the ideal rarely happens with any real consistency. There are seasons where I seem to ebb and flow in the strength of my relationship with Jesus. But this I have learned, even during the times when our hearts may feel weak and less sensitive to God, he still intends to use us for his purpose and glory.

Learning to intersect with others did not come naturally. I grew up in a family where my sanctification was primarily focused around the basic premises of what to avoid, who *not* to hang around with, and what *not* to do. I didn't see that I had a personal responsibility to be engaged with, and to bless and serve others. I was much more in tune to sinful, contaminating behaviors in others and thought it safer and even more spiritual to shun and separate myself from them than to accept the place that God has led them to in their own journey.

I recall a time many years ago when I was asked to join several of my coworkers for an outing of trap shooting followed by beer and pizza at a nearby sports bar. I was truly torn on what to do. My upbringing taught me to stay clear of these fellows who smoked, drank, and were a little too loud and carousing. These were guys I typically would not have hung around with, but something inside told me go for it. I am not sure anything "spiritual" came out of that evening. I shot a pretty good round of trap, turned down the cigars, drank one beer, and rushed home. I have no idea if any one of those fellows became followers of Jesus, but I know that God used that time for his purpose. It was a pivotal step for me in my own life. I began to see the need to

> As best I can see, I believe part of my role is serving as a steward and shepherd of the organization that God has charged me to oversee and manage.

broaden our circle of friends and acquaintances. God was calling me to accept rather than avoid relationships. This was to be a very practical and prophetic calling.

Several years later I started a new company, and through that experience I began to see the extraordinary value our heavenly Father places on relationships. For me personally, it became a matter of understanding more of the gracious nature of God's heart toward all whom he is calling to himself.

For the past fifteen years I have been honored and blessed to serve as a CEO and co-owner of a large midwestern commercial construction company. As best I can see, I believe part of my role is serving as a steward and shepherd of the organization that God has charged me to oversee and manage. As we started the firm, we were determined to create a different kind of construction company, one that was built on core values and was more mission-minded than profit-driven.

Three values were ultimately established: integrity, performance, and relationships. One of my roles as CEO is making sure we live out those values day to day. This has afforded me the opportunity to engage in building relationships within the four corners of the organization as well as in the community at large.

I have heard it said that people are your best asset; in my mind they are your only asset. Early on in the life of the company, I tended to see our team as simply a pipeline for getting things done. Sure I knew the team was critically important to the success of our company, but only through God's grace did I start seeing my associates in a new light. The way we managed our company had a direct impact on their lives. When I viewed them only as coworkers, my impact was less critical to their individual lives. Now I realized that our actions as leaders within the company affected them in a more dramatic fashion. They had families to care for, mortgages to pay, responsibilities and lives outside of our four walls. It wasn't an option anymore to have anything but genuine relationship with these folks. I had to appreciate that they are real people on a real journey themselves.

My spiritual assignment has become that of fellow traveler more than leader of the caravan and self-proclaimed "special assistant" to the Holy Spirit. I freely admit that I still wavier in my relationships. I still struggle not to see them as merely a means to an end but to view every interaction as a divine appointment that gives me the opportunity to be light and salt, to help, to serve, and to encourage others in their journey of faith.

Let me help paint a picture of who I am and how I try to have God work through me. I am not a leader who publically spiritualizes every aspect of my work. I rarely quote the Bible in the office, and I don't wear a witnessing T-shirt in the gym or bring up Jesus in every conversation. Instead, I try to simply be open to what God is doing in the lives of the associates and attempt to see, hear, and be sensitive to his voice. As a leader, my life intersects my associates' lives every day. To the best of my abilities, I try to allow the Holy Spirit to bear his fruit in me and through me. I hope that the associates sense, feel, and taste the goodness of God. I desire to be a good listener, provide clear direction, and give God-inspired encouragement and leadership. I wait for a door to be open and then to speak God's blessing and word to the occasion.

There was such an occasion recently at the office. There was a young associate named John in our company that I often engaged in conversation. He was one of those fellows that did not seem to be intimidated by conversing with the boss. We talked work-related matters, sports, sometimes just what we did over the weekend. I always prayed for an opportunity to share my faith with him, but I would wait for an open door. One day John stepped into my office, sat down, and asked if I had a moment to talk. He told me he went home the night before only to find out that his wife was leaving him.

The waiting was over. The door was wide open. Romans 2:4 tells us that God's kindness leads us to repentance. I wanted God's kindness to show through me. I listened, consoled John, and shared just a few thoughts about life and the Lord. Finally, after sometime, I told John I would pray for him and wanted to follow up with him over the next several weeks. God was in that conversation. As I tried to practice loving my neighbor (fellow associate in this case), John was stirred to become a more consecrated follower of Jesus. It was not a moment to instruct, but a moment to come along side John as a fellow traveler. That was a divinely appointed opportunity for us to walk together on that leg of his journey.

I try to take this same kind of attitude with those in the broader community. I love to cycle, and last summer I considered joining a cycling club. The struggle between avoidance or engagement with the world was pressing on me again, and after some consideration I thought it best to join a group of cyclist that had nothing to do with Christianity. My mental process was simple. I had the chance to engage with those who either don't know the Lord at all or those that may be on a journey in connecting to the Lord. Do we avoid those around us who appear to be so "worldly," or do we jump in and allow the Holy Spirit to guide us in our relationships? We often have a choice.

I am convinced this calling to build relationships in the community is in many ways a divine calling to serve the marketplace. As CEO of the company, many audiences and doors of service have been opened. I have chosen to purposely engage with the art community through

> Do we avoid those around us who appear to be so "worldly," or do we jump in and allow the Holy Spirit to guide us in our relationships? We often have a choice.

serving on boards of art organizations and supporting several art initiatives. My community relationships have opened platforms to speak in various public arenas, and I use those occasions to share my heart and my perspectives publicly to the unbelieving community. It has also allowed me to speak with complete openness at those quasi-secular civic events such as the Mayor's Prayer Breakfast or fundraising events for numerous worthy causes. My work in the community serving humanitarian needs such as our local children's hospital or an educational program for disadvantaged students allows me to clearly state that I value people because my God did so first. It is my prayer that others may taste of God's grace, love, and even his own divinely creative nature through these moments. I am trusting that the fruits of the Holy Spirit are being brought forth in all of these circumstances for others to see and hopefully by faith enjoy the goodness of God.

Of this I am certain, God is calling us into the darkness to be light. Our God is a relational God. He is asking us to engage in relationships to extend his Kingdom, to touch lives, to bless others on their journey, and to potentially alter the eternal course of those we encounter on every step of our path as we journey along together in life. If we can only walk with others in a relationship of divine love, then the Holy Spirit is delighted to light the road with *his* lantern, and we don't ever need to worry about falling along the way.

> Of this I am certain, God is calling us into the darkness to be light. Our God is a relational God. He is asking us to engage in relationships to extend his Kingdom, to touch lives, to bless others on their journey, and to potentially alter the eternal course of those we encounter on every step of our path as we journey along together in life.

IMAGINE...

The thesis for this little book can be summarized in this one statement: "God has a better life for us than the one we are living." This better life is waiting for us every day. This book is our way or inviting you to embrace the height, breadth, and depth of that life. Can you imagine it?

Imagine immersing yourself in the HEIGHT of intimacy with God.

Imagine living each day in a relationship with God that is so real that you can sense his presence as closely as your own breath.

Imagine the fruits of the Spirit flowing effortlessly through you and blessing the lives of everyone you encounter.

Imagine knowing with absolute assurance that Christ will welcome you into his presence with the words "Well done, good and faithful servant," not because of what you have done, but because of what you have allowed him to do in and through you.

Imagine losing yourself in the BREADTH of the freedom of the faithful steward.

Imagine living every day with the amazing peace that comes to the heart of the faithful steward who has stepped off the throne and given control of everything back to its rightful owner.

Imagine being set free from your fears, stress, anxiety, and dread and truly living fully for Christ.

Imagine experiencing the joy of the generous life and the contentment that flows from a heart that is rich toward God.

Imagine committing yourself to the DEPTH of redeemed relationships.

Imagine having a vision for the people around you that allows you to embrace their stories with joy and serve them with selfless service.

Imagine being given the privilege of seeing God do amazing things in the lives of the people you love through your own commitment to journey with them in loving grace.

Imagine how God might change you as you open yourself up to others that he will bring to walk with you in your own journey.

This is the life of the three-dimensional disciple of Jesus Christ! Can you imagine it for yourself?

I have asked my fellow authors to each share with you a closing thought about how you can make this three-dimensional life your own.

CLOSING THOUGHTS

From Melinda…

Since I wrote my chapter for this book, I have transitioned out of the management of Care Net and am currently serving as Care Net's President Emeritus. I now have the opportunity to consult with local pregnancy centers and other faith-based nonprofit organizations as a partner with The Artios Institute. The lessons of abiding in Jesus and bearing fruit continue to amaze me.

As I transitioned out of the management of Care Net, God began to open doors for ministry with organizations in other states and cities. At the same time he also gave me a very clear conviction that I was not to forget my own home-town. I had spoken with several board members working with our local pregnancy center and realized they were in a time of transition and rebuilding for the future. I was not at all clear about what I could help them with, but it was clear to me that I should request a meeting with their full board of directors and just talk with them.

Let's just say that my presentation to that board was not

the intelligent, concise, articulate presentation of an experienced consultant. I usually have a clear outline of concepts and ideas in my head before I speak. Not this time. I sounded unprepared and inarticulate about why or how I could serve them. The only concept that I was clear about was the opportunity for them to build partnerships in the city. The board members were also confused. They could not understand what I could do either.

The next week their new executive director and several board members met me for lunch. As we talked, we all gained some clarity. I could help the director as a mentor and as a consultant with strategic messaging, building relationships, and resource development. The idea of partnership came up again when the director told me that the pastor of a large African American church in town was devoting an entire Sunday evening service to the ministry of the pregnancy center.

That was very encouraging news. The idea of a ministry partnership was taking form, and the service was a generous way of building relationships and bringing God's people together around the issue of life. However, we were totally unprepared for what God was planning for that evening church service.

We watched that Sunday night as almost eight hundred people took their seats in the sanctuary. This congregation was amazing! They knew the facts and statistics about abortion in their community and the nation. There were testimonials, songs, poetry, and words from women and men in the congregation who had participated in an abortion. Some were telling their story for the first time.

This church had dedicated the entire offering that evening to the pregnancy center. The pastor had contacted other churches in the area, and they had sent gifts. He and the deacons and elders each made personal gifts. Then we watched as the vast majority of church members rose from their seats and stood in line to bring their offerings for the pregnancy center. There were entire families in that line. In decades of pro-life ministry, I have never seen a service with such commitment from so many people. Many of those checks were for $25.00 or $50.00. At the end of the evening, that church had given over $20,000 to help women and babies!

The gifts were wonderful, but more wonderful were the hearts of the people in that church and their desire to honor God and work together to protect life. The pregnancy board and director are now working with the pastor and his staff to build a new pregnancy ministry outreach together.

God is at work in our city. We did not produce this fruit. God spoke to this pastor when one of the pregnancy center's volunteers, a member of his congregation, came to his office to tell him the facts about abortion. He knew their church had to act, and he called the center. The pregnancy center board and executive director were praying each week for God to lead them in new directions. God impressed upon me the need to speak to the board, even though I did not know what to say.

To all of us, he gave us the thought of partnerships. God was putting together a pathway and a partnership that will save unborn lives and heal women's hearts. Now I can bring this center together with others across the country that are doing pregnancy ministry in urban communities. They now have access to Care Net's urban resources and a connection to new friends around the country.

> We abide, trust, and listen, and God produces the fruit. We have the joy to be the bearers of that fruit. There is such peace and freedom in "bearing" what God causes to happen.

None of us involved "produced" this fruit. We were all listening, waiting, and trusting God to show us the way. When he impressed us to do something, we did it. This new partnership was not the result of our work for God. It was not anything we could have done on our own. The results I have shared are very dramatic, and every ministry situation is different. But the pathway for us is always the same. We abide, trust, and listen, and God produces the fruit. We have the joy to be the bearers of that fruit. There is such peace and freedom in "bearing" what God causes to happen. I must be honest. This way of trusting, listening, and abiding does not happen often enough in my life. Again, it is God's love that makes me want to see it happen more. This is the abundant life he has promised all of us.

From Bill...

What is the key to experiencing the freedom to become a steward-leader? What is the key to being released from the deep-seated desire to own and control?

I think the key really starts with answering the question of what is the object of your affections. Matthew 13:44 says, "The kingdom of heaven is like treasure hidden in a field, which a man found and covered up. Then in his joy he goes and sells all that he has and buys that field." The story illustrates a simple truth. The man was willing to let go of all of his possessions in exchange for a greater possession: heaven. With the letting go of his possessions, he experiences joy.

I think that all of us want to experience joy. We want the abundance, the unbridled freedom of living life to the maximum. But we'll never get to experience that joy unless we stop and ask ourselves what is our greatest joy. Where do we spend our time? When we have time to daydream, where do our thoughts drift? If they are consumed with what we own, what we may own, or what we may grow, it is likely time to let go of what we have.

I hope that my free thoughts drift heavenward, of my hope in heaven, of my greater joy. That is the exchange we must all make.

In my own story, the harder I tried the less happy I became. I made others around me unhappy, including my children. But when I was forced to finally let go of my desire to own and control, that's when I experienced joy. Indeed, when I saw my role as merely a steward, God began to open up entire new vistas of ministry—Bible studies, opportunities to witness, even a brand new career.

> I think that all of us want to experience joy. We want the abundance, the unbridled freedom of living life to the maximum. But we'll never get to experience that joy unless we stop and ask ourselves what is our greatest joy.

I shudder to think what would have happened if I had held on. So as you consider your own journey of three-dimensional discipleship, let me encourage you to literally and figuratively take out the titles to your cars, your house, your business, or your ministry. Make a complete list of anything you might think you have ownership, and from there, write out a transfer of ownership to the Lord. Give it to him. Let it go, and celebrate the joy of owning nothing—other than Christ.

After you've made this ownership transfer, tell someone about it. Let them know. Let them keep you accountable. I've got a friend who meets with a group of accountability partners, and they actually pull out tax returns and financial statements. They challenge each other to give away ownership interests in companies in order to keep their net worth lower and their giving at higher levels.

That may seem radical. But I know of no other antidote to ownership and greed than the amazing power of letting go. And it is only in letting go that we find freedom and joy.

From Pat...

As we learn to recognize the reality of sojourning with others, we appreciate the beauty of walking alongside both the believing and the non-believing travelers of life...they are all our neighbors. We see that all of us are being affected by the relationships we have with one another. We are accompanied by the Holy Spirit on every step of our journey as we live this reality out with others. We are able to appreciate the personal investment that others are making in our own lives, and we relish the potential of being used by God to be a positive and potentially eternal influence on the lives of those around us.

Since writing my chapter of this book, I have had fresh insights into the meaning of loving my neighbor as myself. My journey has taken on an increasingly intentional direction. I find I am more keenly attuned, more sensitive to times when my path is intersecting with someone else's, and I am accepting greater responsibility for my personal accountability for these moments. These encounters with others aren't simply insignificant moments in time that fleet away. They are windows of opportunity to bear the fruit of God's Spirit and watch it potentially alter the course of life forever.

In the business world, we are constantly analyzing our ROI (return on investment). My prayer for myself and for you is that every aspect of our journey into three-dimensional discipleship will produce a maximum return of the Son's sacrificial investment in us. I pray that our relationships may cause our Lord to beam with delight and joy as an adoring father watching his children grow into full maturity in him.

> In the business world, we are constantly analyzing our ROI (return on investment). My prayer for myself and for you is that every aspect of our journey into three-dimensional discipleship will produce a maximum return of the Son's sacrificial investment in us.

From Scott...

I pray that you will follow these wise words from my three colleagues who have journeyed, and continue to journey, the path of the three-dimensional disciple of Jesus Christ.

I pray that you will submit yourself to God as a branch to a vine, depending on that vine for your very life, and through its nourishment bearing abundant fruit in every season.

I pray that you will be set free to live with the heart of a steward, joyfully obedient to the true owner of everything.

And I pray that you may be granted the vision to see people as God sees them and lovingly enter into their journey as a fellow traveler on the road to your transformation into the image of Christ.

That is discipleship in three dimensions. It brings richness and vitality to our life and will draw all people to Christ through us. We will leave you with a list of these three dimensions and some key Bible verses for you to remember, and with a prayer of the three-dimensional disciple. May it become your prayer!

Discipleship in the First Dimension: Submission. We are Branches Abiding in the Vine.

> *"If you remain in me and I remain in you, you will bear much fruit…this is to my Father's glory that you bear much fruit…fruit that will last."* (John 15:1–17).
>
> *"The fruit of the Spirit is love, joy, peace, patience, kindness, goodness, faithfulness, gentleness, self-control"* (Galatians 5:22–23).

Discipleship in the Second Dimension: Freedom. We are Stewards, not Owners.

> *"The spirit that flows through us brings freedom"* (2 Corinthians 3:17–18).

"It is for freedom that Christ has set us free" (Galatians 5:1).

"Seek first the kingdom of God and his righteousness, and all these things will be added to you" (Matthew 6:33).

Discipleship in the Third Dimension: Journey. We are Fellow Travelers.

"Love the Lord your God with all your heart…and love your neighbor as you love yourself" (Matthew 22:37–40).

"The Lord does not look at the things people look at… the Lord looks at the heart" (1 Samuel 16:7).

"Jesus stopped and ordered the man to be brought to him…" (Luke 18:40).

Prayer

"Dear Lord, help me live today as a branch fully dependent on you, the vine, to nurture and support me, that I might bear in my life the fruit of the Spirit;

Dear Lord, help me to step off my throne and yield everything to you, the true owner, and set me free to steward what you have entrusted to me with joyful obedience;

Dear Lord, help me to see my neighbor as you see them. Use me to bring blessing into their lives and equip me to live as a co-traveler with everyone I meet.

This is my heart's desire, Lord, that you will live in me and through me. In Jesus name, amen!"

About the Authors

Scott Rodin

Scott Rodin is president of Rodin Consulting, Inc. specializing in helping Christian non-profits take a biblical approach to strategic planning, board development and capital campaign fundraising. For twenty-nine years he has served as counsel, coach and trainer to not-for-profits organizations in the U.S., Canada, Middle East, Great Britain, China and Australia.

Dr. Rodin is past president of the Christian Stewardship Association and of the Eastern Baptist Theological Seminary in Philadelphia. He is a Senior Fellow of the Association of Biblical Higher Education and serves on the boards of ChinaSource and the Evangelical Environmental Network.

Dr. Rodin holds Master of Theology and Doctor of Philosophy degrees in Systematic Theology from the University of Aberdeen, Scotland. His books include,

- *The Million-Dollar Dime* (Kingdom Life Publishing, 2012)
- *The Third Conversion* (Kingdom Life Publishing, 2011)
- *The Steward Leader* (InterVarsity Press, 2010)

- *The Sower* (ECFA, 2009)
- *The Four Gifts of the King* (Kingdom Life Publishing, 2008)
- *The Seven Deadly Sins of Christian Fundraising* (Kingdom Life Publishing, , 2007)
- *Abundant Life* (Steward Publishing, 2004)
- *Stewards in the Kingdom* (InterVarsity Press, 2000)

Scott is married to Linda and they reside in Spokane, Washington. Contact him at: scott@rodinconsultinginc.com.

Blog: wp.kingdomlifepublishing.com

Melinda Delahoyde,

A lifelong leader in the pregnancy center movement, Melinda Delahoyde most recently served as President of Care Net, the national affiliation organization for over 1,100 pregnancy centers across the country. She is the author of *Fighting for Life* and her articles on abortion and bioethics have appeared in publications such *Christianity Today, Moody Monthly, Outcomes,* and *Christian Life.* Melinda also serves as a spokesperson on life issues and building a culture of life in America. She has been quoted by the Associated Press, *TIME, WORLD Magazine,* the Salem Radio Network, and has appeared on The 700 Club and the Annenberg Media Channel series, "Ethics in America."

Melinda also serves as a consultant for non-profit organizations on the topics of board governance, resource development and strategic planning and is a partner in The Artios Institute, helping Christian leaders personally and professionally steward the gifts and talents God has given them for His Kingdom.

Melinda is a member of the Board of Directors of the Evangelical Council for Financial Accountability (ECFA) and Southeastern Baptist Theological Seminary. She graduated from the University of California with a B.A. in Philosophy and an M.A, in Philosophy of Religion from Trinity Evangelical Divinity School. She and her husband have four children and live in Raleigh, North Carolina.

William (Bill) High

William (Bill) High is the Chief Executive Officer of National Christian Foundation Heartland. He works with families, individual givers, and financial advisors, sharing the foundation's message regarding biblical generosity and charitable giving. Much of that work includes advising on issues of income tax planning, business sale planning, real estate and estate planning. Bill assists families in documenting their family vision and creating mission statements.

Bill is also the founder of iDonate.com, a fundraising software company serving the non-profit community. iDonate. com provides an online marketing solution for non-profits to market and receive gifts of all kinds, including cash, text, credit card and non-cash gifts. He is also the founder of Christian Foundation Grants, a member based service available to Christian non-profits and churches.

Bill is the President of Generous Life, a legacy consulting organization with the aim of making generosity generational. He is also a published author and conference speaker. He is the general editor of Grants and More for Christian Ministries, and a contributing author to Why the Conservative Mind Matters. He is currently working on three books soon to be published: *Stories of the Generous Life, Revolution in Fundraising,* and The *7 Generation Legacy.*

Prior to joining the National Christian Foundation Heartland in 2000, Bill was a partner with the law firm of Blackwell Sanders LLP, a national and international law firm. He remains Of Counsel with the law firm Sanders Warren & Russell LLP.

Bill has been married to his wife Brooke for twenty-five years. They have four children: Ashley, Jessica, Nathan, and Joseph.

Pat McCown

Pat McCown is Chief Executive Officer and co-founder of McCownGordon Construction, one of the largest general contractors in the Midwest region. Founded upon the core values of Integrity, Performance and Relationships, the firm specializes in various markets including civic, research and development, science and technology, higher education, corporate and healthcare. McCownGordon is committed to providing a high level of professional construction services based on a values-driven philosophy, entrepreneurial atmosphere and distinctive approach to client service. McCownGordon has been named one of the Best Places to Work in Kansas City for the past nine consecutive years by the *Kansas City Business Journal.*

Pat currently serves as Vice Chair of Hillcrest Covenant Church in Prairie Village, Kansas, and is on a number of civic and philanthropic boards in Kansas City, some of which include serving as Trustee for the University of Missouri - Kansas City and the Kansas City Art Institute. He and his wife Beth are both actively involved with numerous other charitable organizations throughout the Kansas City area. In addition to McCown's personal civic service, McCownGordon has a policy of reinvesting at least ten percent of after-tax profits in the Kansas City philanthropic community. The firm was recently named Business Philanthropist of the Year by Nonprofit Connect.

Pat holds a Bachelors Degree in Engineering and a Masters in Business Administration. He resides in Leawood, Kansas, with his wife Beth and is the father to four children and the proud grandfather of four grandchildren.

To order Scott Rodin's books
visit Kingdom Life Publishing at
www.kingdomlifepublishing.com

The Third Conversion

The Million Dollar Dime

The Steward Leader

The Sower

The Four Gifts of the King

The Seven Deadly Sins of Christian Fundraising

*Abundant Life: Experiencing Freedom and Joy
as a Steward of God*

Stewards in the Kingdom